WOMEN AND WORK
an
international
comparison

MARJORIE GALENSON

ILR Paperback No. 13

*N.Y. STATE
SCHOOL OF INDUSTRIAL
& LABOR RELATIONS,
CORNELL
UNIVERSITY*

1973

Price: paper, $3.25
Paper copies bound in cloth, $4.50

ORDER FROM

Publications Division

New York State School of

Industrial and Labor Relations, Cornell University,

Ithaca, New York 14850

Library of Congress Catalog Card Number: 72-619725

ISBN: 0-87546-049-6

PRINTED IN THE UNITED STATES OF AMERICA
BY ONONDAGA PRINTING, INC.

CONTENTS

Tables and Chart

To Emily and Alice
—and Walter and David

Acknowledgements

While collecting data on women in foreign labor markets, I incurred many debts which are a pleasure to acknowledge: to Gisela Emmerij and Minnie Lie, who supplied material and solved some problems of translation and interpretation of data particularly for Holland, Norway, and Sweden; to Veronica Roberts, who facilitated research on Britain; and to officials of the social ministries of Norway, France, and Denmark, and the Swedish National Labor Market Board, all of whom answered requests quickly and generously. Several colleagues in the Department of Consumer Economics and Public Policy at the New York State College of Human Ecology read the manuscript. I am particularly grateful to Professor Emeritus Mabel Rollins, Professor Ethel Vatter, and Dr. Jean Robinson whose suggestions improved the soundness and clarity of the exposition, although I did not always accept their views and I alone am responsible for any errors that remain. Professor Lewis Bower contributed the delightful quotation from de Toqueville at the head of the first chapter. Professors Robert Aronson, Frank Miller, and Vladimir Stoikov of the New York State School of Industrial and Labor Relations read the manuscript and suggested both sources and variables that I had overlooked. I should also like to record a debt that goes back many years: to Hilda Sidney Krech whose book on American women's problems, written long before Women's Liberation, helped to clarify my own experience of the conflicts of educated women.

I am grateful to the New York State College of Human Ecology for a grant from its research funds. Publication of this volume was made possible by the Manpower Research Program under institutional grant number 31-34-70-02 from the Manpower Administration, United States Department of Labor. Points of view or opinions in this publication do not necessarily represent an official position or policy of the Department of Labor.

My daughter Alice carefully checked the manuscript for archaisms. My greatest debt, finally, is to my husband, who not only read the manuscript critically several times but also provided the judicious applications of goad and support that were absolutely essential at every stage of the undertaking.

Marjorie Galenson
New York State College of Human Ecology,
Cornell University

CHAPTER 1   INTRODUCTION

> *". . . I do not hesitate to avow that although the women of the United States are confined within the narrow circle of domestic life, and their situation is in some respects one of extreme dependence, I have nowhere seen woman occupying a loftier position; and if I were asked, now that I am drawing to the close of this work, in which I have spoken of so many important things done by the Americans, to what the singular prosperity and growing strength of that people ought mainly to be attributed, I should reply: To the superiority of their women."*
>
> *Alexis de Toqueville,*
> **Democracy in America.**

Are women in the United States better off than women in other countries? Historically, American women have been considered—both by Americans and by foreigners—to occupy the most favored position and enjoy the highest status of women anywhere. Recently, however, Women's Liberation adherents have contended that the position of American women is inferior not only to that of American men, but also to that of women in many other countries.

We have been told that women in Sweden have complete equality—in contrast to their American counterparts—that Swedish fathers and mothers work part-time in a tandem arrangement so that they can share the task of taking care of the children. We have heard impressive statistics—three-quarters of the doctors in the Soviet Union are women;

women are 50 percent of university students in Finland; half of all women in West Germany are employed—suggesting that American women lag far behind in the quest for equality. It is instructive, then, to look at the facts, to investigate the status of women in European countries through the analysis of labor-market data—how many women work, what kind of employment they have, and how their earnings compare with men's—and information on other aspects of women's working lives such as their education and training, their aspirations, and their general attitudes toward their jobs.

We shall see that some of the stories circulating about other countries are completely false, others are wildly exaggerated, and the rest are true but not conclusive. No one index of women's status, it will appear, can alone characterize a complex of sometimes contradictory social and economic factors. The labor-force participation rate of women is often taken as an index of women's position by Women's Liberation partisans, on the assumption that a high rate is a necessary, if not a sufficient, condition for equality. We will not need to go into the merits of the assumption, fortunately, because we simply do not know what most women think on this question and one would expect that to be an essential datum. The controversy can be avoided because we can show on statistical grounds that the labor-force participation rate contains ambiguities that make it a much less clear concept than it seems at first glance. A high labor-force participation rate is not invariably associated with progressiveness and a high status for women; just as often it indicates the opposite.

The proportion of women in universities is another index that seems conclusive, until the comparative data are considered. For we find that this percentage is higher in Spain than in the Netherlands, and no one would be rash enough to suggest that the position of women is in fact higher in Spain than in the Netherlands.

Similarly, although the proportion of women in the professions, which include the most prestigious and desirable jobs in every country, will tell us a good deal about the status of women, these percentages must nevertheless be looked at not in isolation but together with the entire occupational distribution of women. If we did not, we would assume that nowhere is the status of women higher than in India, Ceylon, and Israel which all have women prime ministers.

Discrimination or Choice?

A comparative study of other countries might be expected, with luck, to throw some light on another controversial question: is women's inferior status in the labor market a result of discrimination, of natural inclination (for "women's jobs"), or of sociological conditioning? Perhaps the evidence from other countries will at least clarify some of the issues involved.

The following pages will present a picture that differs in details—sometimes important details—from country to country, but suggests that conditions affecting women are basically the same all over the West and in Eastern Europe. Even the Soviet Union turns out to be less different than we might have expected. We shall see that women can perform any type of work; somewhere or at some time they have done every type of work that men perform. Nevertheless, women typically work in a narrow range of "women's occupations," rather than across the entire range of occupations. The "women's occupations" are usually the least skilled and always low paid. This common pattern can be traced further back, being foreshadowed in differences in the curricula of boys and girls in school.

In the European countries, girls have less schooling at the secondary level than boys. The boys are more likely to study science, pure and applied, and mathematics; and the girls have begun to gravitate to the arts, particularly languages and literature. The proportions of the sexes enrolled in school begin to diverge seriously after the secondary level: a much higher proportion of the boys take vocational training and apprenticeships, and many more of them enter universities (except in Finland). In the universities, the girls concentrate on arts subjects and tend to drop out more than boys do, so that their proportion among graduates is lower than among entering students. The boys enter fields of applied science and engineering in much greater numbers—with the single exception of the Soviet Union, where almost one-third of the engineering students are girls.

After finishing school, almost every boy takes a job. Not all girls do; some marry and do not seek employment. Everywhere, however, women university graduates are much more likely to work than less-educated women, and the professionally trained (doctors, lawyers) have the highest employment rate of all women.

A sharp drop in women's employment comes with marriage or, more often, with the birth of the first child. The fact that women have traditionally left the labor market at this point suggests that their reluctance to enter long-term training programs is pragmatically justified: such an investment of time and money would have a very short pay-off period (32:45). In the midfifties, a movement on the part of middle-aged women back into the labor market emerged in the most advanced countries. Most recently, the second peak is expanding, evening out, as young mothers continue to work in increasing numbers through the infancy of their children. This trend, if it continues, may in time change the whole picture of female employment, but it is too soon to tell.

Women have many disabilities in the labor market. The fact that they usually leave their jobs at marriage, or when they have children, operates to reduce both their ambition and their employer's interest in promoting them to more responsible jobs or giving them on-the-job training. At work, employers claim that women are absent more often than men; and they are less mobile, for family reasons, whether married or unmarried. For the women reentering the labor market in middle age, the chances of getting a good job have diminished, because whatever skills they possessed have become rusty. To complete the picture, we shall see that the great majority of women who have household responsibilities need to spend several hours a day at them and thus, if these women are employed, work a substantially longer number of hours per week than do men.

Outside the place of work and outside the home women are rarely active or even represented. In all countries, union activities and, most important of all, political activities remain male bailiwicks.

There seems to be sufficient reason in the life cycle of the average woman to explain her inferior job status. Not even the experience of other countries can throw any light on the fundamental question of whether women are "different" from men for biological reasons or because of social conditioning, because nowhere, not even in the Soviet Union, are all the social forces the same for both sexes. The experience of other countries, however, can help us with some questions, such as: (1) Are women actually less reliable employees, or is this another stereotype without real basis in fact? (2) Why do so few women, all over the world, hold down top jobs? What do they consider the reason for their lower status, and what do their male colleagues think? Do we have a clue in the fact that women who get to the top are more likely to be single or, if married, to have one child? (3) why do women in the Soviet Union, where education and training are almost identical for boys and girls, fail to reach the top in numbers proportional to their representation in the professions?

It is interesting and instructive to learn that, even in Russia, women do not want the more responsible jobs with worries that they cannot leave behind at the end of the day. In Sweden the government has accepted the views of intellectuals that sex-differentiation roles must be broken down early, starting in the elementary schools; and some couples are experimenting with sharing part-time work and housework, but this arrangement in fact is not common "owing to the prejudices still surrounding the role of the father in taking care of the children" (72:55). It is interesting to note the observation of a British writer that women are disadvantaged in rising to the top by the absence of any equivalent for women of the "old boy network," because academic women in the United States have been found to be hampered by the same lack (3). In the Soviet Union a variant of the same phenomenon was called, by two Russian women, the major obstacle to women's rising to top executive positions: business was typically conducted in a male atmosphere, they reported, with a good deal of drinking—and women were excluded (37:269).

Finally, the results of the attitudinal surveys that have explored women's job satisfaction are also enlightening: the majority of women *are* satisfied with their low-level, low-paid jobs, more so than the men in comparable jobs. The women's expectations were not very high because their main concern was elsewhere, with their home and family. Whatever the facts of "discrimination," this is probably the principal explanation of why women's situation is what it is.

Attitudes and Prejudices

Division of Labor. Fundamental to most people's thinking on the question of women and work is the assumption that there exists in society a division of labor between the sexes. Women have an absolute advantage in bearing children and a comparative advantage in rearing them; those duties and tending the home are their primary social function. Whether they engage in employment outside the home because they choose to, or even if they are compelled to work for economic reasons, home and children are still their first responsibility. It follows from this set of assumptions that training in professional or technical skills not related to work within the home is not important for women, or at least that it is less important than for men. In fact, where such training is expensive, it is positively uneconomic to allocate places to women which could be filled by men because, on the average, women's working lives are shorter than men's. Put in terms of investment in human capital, as many economists view education,[1] the investment is less profitable both for the women them-

[1]For a description of the human capital approach, see Lester Thurow, *Investment in Human Capital* (Belmont, Calif.: Wadsworth Publishing Co., 1970).

selves and for society because the return on the investment has a shorter pay-off period at best and because at worst there may be no pay-off at all. For example, the traditional discrimination of medical schools against women applicants makes good economic sense: facilities for training doctors are limited and expensive; at the same time, the probability that a woman will never practice is greater than for a man.

This set of assumptions describes part of the reality, but not the whole. The greater the amount of training, the better the chances of its paying off; we shall see that highly trained women have very high employment rates. Furthermore, assuming a normal distribution of ability, society may be losing the potential skills of women superior to some percentage of the men now given preferential treatment. Neither does the "division of labor" explain why women doing the same work as men get less pay. Any discussion of women in the labor market must come to terms with the issue of discrimination and with the substance of employers' stereotypes of women workers.

Prejudice. There is no agreement on the contribution of prejudice to the low status of women in employment, on how much of the dual labor market is attributable to it, but of the existence of prejudice there can be no dispute. Both men and women have volunteered the evidence. Very few men today could—or would dare—put it as neatly as Alfred Marshall did in 1888 speaking to Beatrice Webb. About the conversation, she wrote,

It opened with chaff about men and women: he holding that woman was a subordinate being and that, if she ceased to be subordinate, there would be no object for a man to marry. That marriage was a sacrifice of masculine freedom, and would only be tolerated by male creatures so long as it meant the devotion, body and soul, of the female to the male. Hence, the woman must not develop her faculties in a way unpleasant to the man: that strength, courage, independence, were not attractive in women; that rivalry in men's pursuits was positively unpleasant. . . . "If you compete with us we shan't marry you," he summed up with a laugh.[2]

But the personnel manager of a large British firm recently put it just as bluntly: "I'm an Englishman, and I think most people, like me, would never work for a woman or a black."[3]

Women themselves can be seen to be prejudiced against women at work. They engage in the generalizing from particular cases that characteristically dogs minorities of all kinds. For example, women in the British plant of a large international company considered women irritable, ruthless, nagging, and whining, qualities that naturally kept them from getting ahead (14:44-46). One-third of the women in a survey of the British civil service judged women to be less capable of holding the undersecretaryship (14:278). Both men and women believed that the main difficulty was that women were too diffident, although there was ambivalence about this quality; when a woman did display initiative or ambition or otherwise attempted to move up, she was regarded as dangerously aggressive and unpleasant.

The contradictory views on ambitious women, often held at the same time, are amusingly described in the following summary of opinions about women politicians in West Germany (61:44):

1. The woman politician must have a career. She must be able to show that she is capable of achieving something. But she must not be too involved in her career. If she were she would not be a real woman.

2. She must be more capable and more knowledgeable than the average of her male rivals: But she must not show it.

3. She must, of course, have a husband. If she doesn't then she may be suspected of going in for politics because she cannot catch a man.

4. But if she is married then she would do better to look after her husband, since he must usually concern himself with politics.

---

[2]Webb, Beatrice, *My Apprenticeship*, London, 1926, cited in 30:9.
[3]*The Sunday Times* (London), November 21, 1971, p. 65.

5. She must have children, preferably several. If she has no children she may be suspected of concerning herself with politics because she cannot devote herself to her children. But if she does have children why has she entered politics? Why doesn't she look after her children? She must be a bad mother. So how can she be a good politician?

Psychological explanations for prejudices have been advanced in other countries in terms familiar to Americans:

Reason alone cannot explain why women are so jealously excluded from executive dining rooms and why they have to struggle so hard to get into specific occupations (like stockbroking) where the standard of existing male membership is so low. Explanations must come from a deeper level. One is straight primal fear that women in top jobs will castrate the chaps underneath them [11].

In no country is the situation very different. Dodge (10) denies that there is prejudice in the Soviet Union; at least, no man admitted it and none of the women he interviewed asserted it. One suspects, however, that he did not probe sufficiently, because another writer, one long sympathetic to the Soviet Union, has acknowledged that there is "some degree of validity" to the charge that prejudice exists (37:265; see also pp. 80-104 below).

Employers' Complaints. Employers in other countries give the same justifications for the "discrimination" against women workers as those we hear in the United States: higher absenteeism, the discontinuity in their employment, their lack of interest in the work.

Women do tend to be absent more than men, but studies have indicated that this association is a compound of several other effects. First, absenteeism is heaviest among mothers of young children. Fathers do not stay home from work to take care of a sick child, even in the Soviet Union. (In Poland a mother and not the father has the privilege of taking leave to care for sick children, even if his work would permit him to interrupt it more readily.) Second, absenteeism has been found to be a function more of grade than of sex. Swedish data on the relation between the wage level and days lost through sickness indicate clearly that the higher the income, the fewer the number of days lost. The reason may be that persons who are often sick do not advance to the better paying jobs. It may also be, however, that low-paid workers do not find their jobs as interesting and absorbing as the better-paid workers do and are, therefore, more inclined to stay away from work. In Poland women in better jobs took less advantage of the full maternity and sick leaves provided by law. In Sweden, again, the Industrial Institute for Economic and Social Research found that total absenteeism among *salaried* employees in industry was somewhat lower for women; the highest absenteeism was incurred by single parents, both male and female.

Regarding the argument that women are more likely to leave a job, the very opposite may be true. Restrictions on a woman's mobility—because of having to work near her family's or her husband's residence—probably serve to make her a more faithful employee, less likely to leave for a better job elsewhere. The "wastage rate," a study in Sweden revealed, was, in fact, higher for men than for women (54:80-81). A large-scale survey in Great Britain indicated that working women had had 2.1 jobs in the previous ten years, compared with 2.3 jobs for men (25:13). In the aggregate, on the other hand, women do have shorter working lives than men because of lower labor-force participation rates, maternity leaves, less overtime, earlier retirement, as Dodge points out (234).

Experience in other countries suggests that the allegation that women are less interested in their work than men are depends very much on the level of their work. To quote a Swedish source:

It is said, for example, that men take a more positive attitude to and are more absorbed in their work than women. "Evidence" for this statement has also been presented in a number of studies. However, they are all found in studies comparing men and women as a whole in a branch of industry or an enterprise without regard to the type of work or the qualifications required. In a study of female processing workers at "AB Svenska Salpeterverken" at Köping undertaken by the Swedish Council for Personnel Administration, we can read the following:

"In the present study we have had the opportunity of examining a group of female workers in a job previously considered suitable primarily for men and we have been able to compare them with a group of men performing similar tasks. It may be said that one has here broken with the traditional practice of giving the women unqualified jobs and that it has instead been tried to give them more qualified tasks. This has been done after systematic selection followed by a training period in accordance with a special plan.

"A general result of the study is that the women take a more positive attitude to the job than the men. The women like their job better than the men; they find it more interesting and absorbing, and their attitude to supervisors, managers, earnings and information is more positive . . . we find differences between the jobs in the group showing that the more qualified the job is, the higher is the work motivation" [67:5-6].

CHAPTER 2   THE FEMALE LABOR MARKET IN EUROPEAN COUNTRIES

Supply and Demand Factors

One of the products of the substantial economic progress made by all European countries after the devastation of World War II was full employment. The period after 1950, on the whole, was one of rapid growth; in many of the countries a shortage of labor developed. Where free movement was permitted, workers migrated from the labor-surplus Mediterranean countries to the North, from Italy, Spain, Yugoslavia, Greece, and Turkey to West Germany, Belgium, Sweden, France, Great Britain, and Switzerland. The Eastern European countries, on the other hand, could not rely on immigration to supplement their indigenous labor force.

The main internal source of untapped labor in both the East and the West was women. A peculiarity of the population structure in the countries with very heavy war casualties —particularly the Soviet Union and East and West Germany— served to raise further the demand for female workers: an excess of women and a deficit of men in the working-age cohorts that will not have worked its way through the population pyramid until about 1985. East Germany lost, in addition, a substantial number of men through political defections.

Another characteristic of postwar growth was the strong trend toward the services, which included many of the traditional women's occupations: school teachers, nurses, salesclerks, clerical workers.

As a result of the strong demand for labor, activity rates of women—the proportion of women workers to the total female population in the working-age groups[1]—rose, between 1950 and 1965, in seven of the Western countries[2] for which data are available and in most of the Eastern countries.[3] In the few countries where female participation in the labor force declined,[4] the decline was attributable in the main to the contraction of the agricultural sector in which female activity was universal, with farmers' wives being counted automatically as part of the labor force. Thus, in the Soviet Union and France, the overall activity rate of women fell, but their employment *outside* agriculture rose. In West Germany and Austria a large drop in the number of women emloyed in agriculture was more than compensated for by the rise of female employment elsewhere in the economy.

In the Eastern European countries and at least three of the Western—Sweden, Norway, and the United Kingdom—well over half the total increase in the labor force between 1950 and 1965 was contributed by women; in Sweden, women accounted for as much as two-thirds of the increase in the labor force.

Supply of Women Workers. The supply of women entering the labor market had to draw heavily on married women. Young women had always worked in large numbers in every country until marriage, so a rise in the activity rate necessarily required an increase in the employment of married women. Furthermore, after the war, a rise in the marriage rate, and a lowering of the age at marriage, cut into both the supply of unmarried women and the number of years during which they held temporary employment. In most of the countries studied, the proportion of married women in the labor force and the proportion of women workers who were married

[1]Generally, fifteen or sixteen to sixty-five years in the West, fifteen to sixty years in the East.

[2]Austria, Belgium, Norway, Sweden, Switzerland, West Germany, United Kingdom (76:231-35).

[3]E. g., Bulgaria, Czechoslovakia, East Germany, Hungary, and Poland (2:177).

[4]Denmark, Finland, and France in the West; Rumania and the Soviet Union in the East.

rose with each postwar census. (In France, however, this increase did not start until 1962.)

Labor-Force Participation Rates

There are several ways of measuring women's particiation in the labor force, but some general points can be made about all of them. First, a large proportion of women work, not only in the most advanced countries today—for example, the United States and Sweden—but also in some less developed countries. At issue is whether the wives of farmers are counted in the labor force; in most countries they are. Therefore, the less developed countries with substantial agricultural sectors have high female employment rates. As countries develop industrially, the initial response of female employment measures is to fall, along with the decline of the importance of agriculture in the economy. The second stage of development witnesses a rise in women's activity rates. These effects can be seen most recently in France, where the proportion of working women declined until 1962; since then it has been rising.

Second, demographic factors influence labor-participation rates. The imbalance of the sexes attributable to the high wartime casualties in the Soviet Union and East and West Germany, in particular—but also in some of the other Eastern European countries—has led to a large surplus of women of working age in the population. The excess of women would tend, with other things equal, to raise the ratio of women to men in the working population in two ways: directly, of course, but also indirectly because in these age cohorts there will be an abnormally large number of women without husbands and unmarried women always have higher employment rates than married women.

One more caution about a hasty acceptance of labor-force participation rates as an index of "emancipation": every country, except Switzerland, counts part-time workers in the labor force. A very high proportion of women workers, particularly married women, work only part time, for example, in

Sweden over 50 percent, in Great Britain just under 50 percent. In the United States, only 44 percent of all women workers were employed at least thirty-five hours a week for forty-eight weeks or more per year. We are probably aware in our own country that not all the women counted as working in the census surveys are truly dedicated "career women," but it is easy to read the figures referring to foreign countries uncritically, without the necessary qualifications.

The simplest of the percentages cited in Table 1, the percentage of working women aged fifteen to sixty-five years in relation to the total number of women in that age group in the population, is, unfortunately, the least reliable. Not all countries use the same age limits. Furthermore, it is heavily influenced by the average length of time young people stay in school. The American rate is particularly affected because we have the highest proportion of young people in college; hence, the percentage for the United States is lower than it would otherwise be.

Women as a percentage of the labor force, the second index in Table 1, is also influenced by any disparity in the sex ratio of the population, but is less influenced by the proportion of youths still in school, a factor which affects both sexes, although unequally. According to this index, of the countries listed, the United States has relatively more women in the total labor force than even Sweden, being exceeded only by Finland and the Soviet Union.

The next column, the percentage of all *married* women working, is probably the best single index of the commitment of women in a country to employment. Note that West Germany falls to a level significantly below that of the United States, because that high index for all women cited on page 2 is in fact due to the large number of *single* women in the unbalanced middle-age cohorts. Only the three Scandinavian countries (and undoubtedly the Soviet Union, if the data were available) exceed the American level, a fact which accords with our expectations. The surprises in this column are the very low percentages reported for two of the advanced

Western countries, the Netherlands and Norway. The rates are the more puzzling because near neighbors of both, Belgium for the one and Sweden and Denmark for the other, have substantially higher rates. These percentages appear to dispose effectively of the possibility of accepting a high female activity rate as a proxy for the status of women in general.

Participation Rates By Age

As Table 2 shows, the age at which the employment of women generally peaks is from twenty to twenty-four. When they are between school and marriage, approximately half the women of this age group are in the labor force, even in Norway; in the other countries the percentage hovers around 60, and in the Soviet Union it reaches 80 percent. Thereafter, the percentage declines, as women enter the child-bearing years. Only in Sweden does the percentage of women in the labor force rise to a higher rate at any later age, thirty-five to fifty-five years of age for Swedish women. If we had later data for Finland, its curve would probably be as high as the Swedish.

The chart presents the data in graphic form.[5] The two-peaked curve appears clearly: the pattern of women in the more advanced countries returning to the labor market after their children are grown. That is the first stage. The next stage can be seen in the curves for Sweden, Finland, and the United States: The gradual evening out as women in their twenties continue working after marriage and children so that the second peak gradually turns into a plateau. Compare the American curves for the two census dates 1960 and 1970.

Occupational Distribution

Roughly two-thirds to three-quarters of women workers in the countries listed in Table 3 were employed in services; the proportion was lower only in the countries with a substantial number of women still employed in agriculture.

Women account for about half the sales workers in most of the countries in Table 4 and for an even higher proportion, on

[5]Data in this chart are from the sources cited in Table 2.

Chart. Labor-Force Participation Rates of Women by Age

LABOR FORCE PARTICIPATION RATES OF WOMEN BY AGE

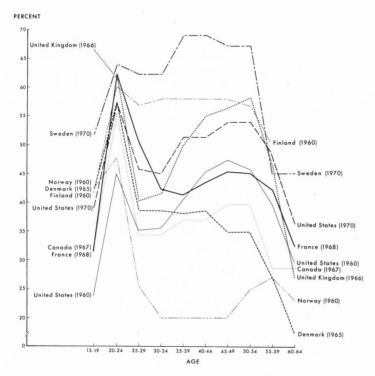

the whole, of the clerical workers. Service workers were almost three-quarters women; this category includes mainly domestic servants and other cleaning staff.

The category of administrative, executive, and managerial workers includes no more than one-fifth women in any country. Among craftsmen and production workers, the highest proportion of women is also one-fifth; most of these are unskilled and semiskilled workers. There are substantial numbers of skilled women workers only in textiles and clothing, industries that are contracting in Western Europe. Professional, technical, and related workers comprise a fairly high

Table 1: Women in the Labor Force: Selected Countries

Country	Date	Working women Percent of women 15-65 years	Working women Percent of labor force	Married women in labor force Percent of all married women	Married women in labor force Percent of female labor force
Belgium	1966		30.8		
	1961	25.8		20.5	52.2
Canada	1968		34.0	30.0	54.6
	1961	29.7			
Denmark	1969		38.0	47.0	60.3
	1965	37.7(a)			
Finland	1968		43.0	60.0	60.4
	1960	35.0(b)			
France	1968	43.5		37.8	
	1967		31.9		
	1962				53.2
Germany (F.R.)	1967	47.0(c)		33.3	53.2
	1966		36.7		
Great Britain	1969		35.8	39.3	59.6
	1966	42.3			
Italy	1966		26.9		
	1965				21.8
Netherlands	1960	22.6	22.3	7.0	
Norway	1960	23.8(d)	22.9	9.5	
Sweden	1970	53.7(e)	40.0(e)	52.7	63.2
Switzerland	1965		28.9		
	1960	38.9		16.0	25.0

United States	1970	42.6[c]	41.3	40.8	60.0
USSR	1965	79.0[g]	52.0		50.0

[a] Age 14 and over.
[b] All ages.
[c] Date uncertain.
[d] Age 15 and over.
[e] Age 16 through 74.
[f] Age 16 and over.
[g] Age 16 to 55.

Sources: International Labor Organization, Organization for Economic Cooperation and Development, country statistical yearbooks and censuses.

Table 2: Women's Labor-Force Participation Rates by Age Group: Selected Countries

Country	Year	Age							
		15-19	20-24	25-29	30-34	35-39	40-44	45-49	50-54
Canada	1967	31.6[a]	56.6		34.4		37.0	39.7	
Denmark	1965	42.4[a]	57.4		38.6	38.2	38.7	34.8	
Finland	1960	41.7	60.7	56.9		58.0			56.9
France	1968	31.4	62.4	50.6	42.4	41.3	43.4	45.3	45.1
Germany (F.R.)	1964	69.2	71.7	51.3	43.2	45.1	47.6	45.1	40.6
Great Britain	1966	66.5	61.6	40.4	41.6	50.0	55.2	56.5	53.0
Norway	1960	42.5	47.7	25.6		18.8	21.2		24.9
Sweden	1970	51.9[b]	63.9		62.4	69.2		67.3	
United States	1970	39.2[b]	56.9	45.8	45.0	51.1		54.0	
USSR	1959	62.0	80.3		77.7		75.4		67.4

[a]14-19
[b]16-19

Sources:

Canada: B. N. Seear, Re-entry of Women to the Labor Market (Paris: Organization for Economic Cooperation and Development, 1971), p. 37.

Denmark: Statistiske Department, Population and Housing Census (Copenhagen: Statistiske Departement, 1965), Table 10.

Finland: International Labor Office, Yearbook of Labor Statistics 1969 (Geneva: ILO, 1970), Table 1.

France: Seear, op. cit., p. 59.

Germany (F.R.): Seear, op. cit., p. 50.

Great Britain: Sample Census 1966 (London: HMSO, 1967), Part 1, Table 1.

Norway: International Labor Office, op. cit.

Sweden: Statistiska Centralbyrån, *Statistiska Meddelanden* [Statistical Reports] (Stockholm: National Central Bureau of Statistics, 1971), p. 10.

United States: United States Department of Labor, Bureau of Labor Statistics, *Marital and Family Characteristics of Workers, March 1970*, Special Labor Force Report 130 (Washington: GPO, 1971), p. A-10.

USSR: Berent, J., "Some Demographic Aspects of Female Employment in Eastern Europe and the USSR," *International Labor Review*, February 1970, p. 181.

Table 3: Distribution of Female Labor Force by Sector

Country	Year	Percentage distribution of female labor force by sector			Percentage of women in each sector's total labor force		
		Agriculture	Industry	Services	Agriculture	Industry	Services
Belgium	1961	4.6	31.9	63.5	16.3	18.1	38.2
Canada	1961	4.7	19.4	75.9	10.4	15.5	40.0
Denmark	1960	5.4	24.6	70.0	9.4	20.7	48.5
Finland	1960	31.9	22.0	46.1	35.3	27.5	55.4
France	1962	19.6	26.6	53.8	32.6	23.2	45.8
Germany (F.R.)	1961	19.8	33.5	46.7	54.7	25.5	45.6
Italy	1961	30.8	31.3	37.9	26.3	19.1	31.1
Netherlands	1960	4.4	22.8	72.8	9.1	12.0	34.6
Norway	1960	4.0	22.2	73.8	4.6	13.9	38.7
Sweden	1960	4.0	27.2	68.8	8.7	17.9	50.1
Switzerland	1960	3.0	37.1	59.9	8.2	22.1	47.0
United Kingdom	1961	1.3	35.8	62.9	10.6	24.5	42.1
United States	1960	2.1	24.0	73.9	10.0	20.8	43.3

Source: International Labor Office, "Statistical Information on Women's Participation in Economic Activity," mimeographed (Geneva: ILO, 1970), Table V.

Table 4: Percentage of Women in Total Labor Force in Seven Occupational Groups

Country	Year	Professional, technical, and related workers	Administrative, executive, and managerial workers	Clerical workers	Sales workers	Craftsmen and production workers	Service workers	Farmers, fishermen
Belgium	1961	42.2	8.6	33.9	51.8	17.5	64.3	15.9
Canada	1961	46.6	9.5	61.1	35.1	12.1	55.3	10.0
Denmark	1960	49.2	12.3	60.3	37.8	18.0	79.7	9.2
Finland	1960	48.1	10.3	79.5	60.5	24.5	79.9	35.4
France	1962	43.1	20.9	65.9	52.2	19.8	71.4	32.7
Germany (F.R.)	1961	33.1	20.0	54.9	52.6	21.3	67.9	54.2
Italy	1965	37.1	32.6		34.5	20.1	64.0	32.0
Netherlands	1960	39.2	4.1	35.8	37.0	9.3	64.7	8.7
Norway	1960	37.1	6.7	59.3	44.3	11.2	71.6	4.6
Sweden	1965	39.9	9.0	71.4	48.5	14.7	73.8	22.6
United Kingdom	1966	38.3	7.5	67.3	48.3	20.1	71.0	12.1
United States	1967	37.6	15.8	72.7	42.7	13.1	64.5	17.7

Source: International Labor Office, "Statistical Information on Women's Participation in Economic Activity," mimeographed (Geneva: ILO, 1970), Table VIII.

proportion of women because school teachers are classified in this category.

Professional Occupations. The professions include many of the most interesting and attractive jobs. For women, they have an additional advantage: here women do the same work as men, a situation that exists in few other occupations. Women, however, do not occupy the higher-level jobs in these occupations in proportions anywhere close to their overall participation. The distribution of women forms a pyramid, broad at the base and narrowing toward the top, in these occupations as in all the others. Nevertheless, although equality does not extend up the ladder, it remains true that women are more nearly equal in the professions calling for high skill and training than in the lower-level jobs.

Medicine is the area in which the greatest difference prevails between the United States and the other countries. In country after country, medicine is regarded as one of the traditional women's occupations, as an acceptable extension of women's interests in caring for people. Even in Czarist Russia many girls studied medicine. The United States has by far the lowest proportion of women doctors in Table 5. Most of the other countries have about one-fifth; even Switzerland and Norway have percentages in excess of the American figure.

Table 5: Proportion of Women in Medicine

Denmark	16.4	Norway	10.3
Finland	23.4	Sweden	17.4
France	12.8	Switzerland	13.6
Germany (F.R.)	20.0	United States	6.7
Great Britain	18.0	USSR	75.0
Italy	18.8		

Sources: Censuses (Finland and Norway, 1960; Sweden, 1965; Great Britain, 1966); *Facts on Prospective and Practicing Women in Medicine* (prepared for Conference on Meeting Medical Manpower Needs, co-sponsored by American Women's Medical Association and U.S. Department of Labor, Washington, D.C., January 12 to 13, 1968), p. 40; N. T. Dodge, *Women in the Soviet Economy* (Baltimore: Johns Hopkins, 1966), p. 209. (Figures for France, Denmark, West Germany, Switzerland, and the United States are all for 1965; those for the Soviet Union are for 1963.)

Why is this? Any explanation of the situation—which is improving—must take account of the uniquely powerful position of the American Medical Association. No other national medical association has been so successful in maintaining tight controls over the accreditation of medical schools and over the testing of entrants into the field. For these reasons, and because of political power sufficient to prevent, until recently, any subsidy of medical schools that would increase the supply of doctors, doctors enjoy relatively higher incomes in the United States than in the other countries. (In Russia, with the great majority of doctors women, the profession is relatively low paid.) One suspects that the power of a conservative, economics-oriented trade association such as the AMA would be hostile to any substantial influx of women and that, with their professional and political power, their attitude would be easily translated into admission policies, since there has ordinarily been a great excess supply of applicants to medical schools. Medicine is the principal exception in the occupational picture, the area in which American women are far behind European women. To it might be added two allied professions in which there are large percentages of women practitioners in some of the other countries, dentistry and pharmacy (see Table 6).

Table 6: Women in Dentistry and Pharmacy

	Percentage	
	Dentists	Pharmacists
Denmark	25.0	
Finland	76.9	85.8
Germany (F.R.)	13.0	
Norway	20.1	92.3[a]
Sweden	23.6	68.9
Great Britain	10.6	33.0
United States	1.3	

[a]Pharmacy degrees granted in 1970.

Sources: National Censuses: Finland, 1960; Norway, 1960; Sweden, 1965; Great Britain, 1966; Germany, 1965: Sommerkorn, 45; United States: *The New York Times,* January 31, 1972; Denmark: Sullerot, 271.

There is less difference between the percentage of women lawyers in the United States and that in other countries. Compared with the 2.8 percent for this country in 1971, Great Britain's 5 percent (1966 census) sounds high, but in fact most of the English women lawyers are solicitors and not the more glamorous barristers. Other countries with a higher proportion of women lawyers—between 7 and 8 percent—include Finland, Sweden, Switzerland, and Denmark.

Engineering is one of the most exclusively male professions in every country. Outside the Soviet Union, where one-third of the engineers are women, the highest percentage of women engineers in the West seems to be the 3.6 percent in Finland (1960 census). In Great Britain the proportion of women engineers was 0.4 percent (16), and in Norway, 0.6 percent (24:393).[6]

Vying with engineering as the most exclusively male profession is politics. In six countries, the proportion of women members in the national parliament in the late 1960s was as follows:

Finland	17 percent
Great Britain	4
Norway	9
Sweden (lower house)	14
West Germany	7 to 9
Soviet Union	28

The women at higher political levels, in ministerial posts or in top party jobs, could be counted easily on one hand. The occasional women ministers have usually been in health and welfare or education and culture ministries. Norway has had an outstanding exception, a woman who has been both a member of the central executive committee of a major political party for many years and the president of the parliament.

The rarity of women in politics in the Communist countries, where the Communist party plays such a decisive role in the

---

[6]A wild exaggeration occurs in (51:13) where it is stated that in Norway one out of ten engineers is a woman.

economy, may explain in part the rather disappointing record of women in those countries in reaching the top.

Teaching. Elementary school teaching is a woman's occupation, as Table 7 shows, with women accounting for at least half the total number of teachers in the countries for which we have data. There are smaller percentages of women teachers at the secondary level—again, the pyramid typical of women's employment experiences is evident—and very much smaller percentages at the college and university level. (It should be recalled that secondary school in the European countries includes at least the first year of the American college, and in Great Britain the first two years.)

Table 7: Proportion of Women Teachers

	Elementary	Secondary	University
Austria			8.0
Canada			13.2
Denmark	50.0		
Finland	63.1		17.7
France	66.0	52.0	20.6
Germany (F.R.)	50.8	30.8	2.3
Great Britain	75.0		10.8
Netherlands	52.0	22.0	3.3
Norway	48.9	21.6	1.7
Sweden	74.8	40.0	10.0
United States	85.0	46.0	20.0

Source: National Censuses and the Organization for Economic Cooperation and Development for various dates in the 1960s.

In university teaching, women are concentrated at the lower levels—research associates, instructors, lecturers—and their numbers diminish as the promotional ladder is ascended. This situation holds for every country for which we have data, as we shall see in the country accounts that follow.

It should also be noted that the American figures for university teachers are somewhat inflated, because they cover home economics, education, and library courses—all traditional women's fields—which many European countries do not include in university education.

Students. More young people attend institutions of higher education in the United States than any other country, by far; but only 40 percent of girls attend college. The United States lags behind Finland, France, and the Soviet Union (Table 8). Of the countries for which we have data, Finland has the highest ratio of female enrollment, over 50 percent. In the Soviet Union, the proportion of women university students peaked at 52 percent in 1955, but declined thereafter to a low of 42 percent in 1962; the most recent figure available is 44 percent for 1965.

The smaller proportion of women acquiring higher education tells only part of the story. The poor representation of women in skilled and professional employment can be traced back to the earlier choices made by girls still in school, at least to the secondary level when they began to elect—or in some cases the school or community to elect for them—courses of study that had no clear professional focus. Female participation rates for different fields of study at the university level, shown for various countries in Table 8, indicate the overwhelming preference of women everywhere for the humanities. In general the humanities prepare only for teaching, so women have limited their options before they enter the labor market. Technological subjects attracted the fewest girls. Women were also underrepresented in the social sciences and the natural sciences. In scientific fields, they were more inclined to study biology or chemistry than physics.

Association between Education and Employment. The girls who were outnumbered by men in the universities and who elected to study the humanities, because they either had made no career plans or had opted for the traditional woman's career of teaching, were in fact the select group with respect to employment after graduation. In country after country, we shall find evidence that the more highly educated entered, or reentered, the labor market, whether married or not and whether or not they had children. Professionally trained women were the most likely of all to continue in employment

Table 8: Rate of Female Participation in Universities by Field of Study, Selected OECD Countries, 1965

	Total enrollment	Pure science	Technology	Social sciences	Humanities
Belgium	28.1	27.6	0.9	17.2	45.5
Canada		17.8	0.9	19.1	40.4
Denmark	36.0	22.3	4.2	6.1	50.8
Finland	50.6	36.2	3.7	43.3	75.5
France	45.0	31.0			65.0
Germany (F.R.)	26.0	12.7	0.6	13.4	39.7
Netherlands	18.0	12.3	0.7	12.7	40.5
Norway	25.8	14.6	4.2	8.2	43.0
Spain	21.8	25.7	0.5	16.8	61.2
Sweden	42.0	25.0	5.9	38.3	63.0
United Kingdom	29.0	22.1	1.8	31.1	42.1
United States	40.0	26.1	0.4	24.0	49.7
Yugoslavia	41.1[a]	38.1	12.7	33.5	56.9

[a]At age of highest enrollment.

Sources: OECD, Education Committee, *Development of Higher Education, 1950-1967: Analytical Report* (Paris: OECD, Nov. 9, 1970); various sources for total enrollment.

throughout their active years. This trend has increased over time and is stronger among younger age groups.

It also seems to be true in several countries that career women who work uninterruptedly and reach top jobs are more likely to be single than other women. Which way the causality goes is not entirely clear; one would suspect that it runs both ways. There is evidence, moreover, that successful women who marry are more likely to have no children or one child rather than three or more.

Although a positive association between education and employment has appeared in several surveys in various countries, the older negative association between wives' economic activity rates and husbands' income still holds, because the number of highly educated women is still too small to counter the other effect, which prevails for less-educated women (32:23-24). Two other associations that have been frequently observed in several countries are that as the number of children increases, the labor-force participation rate of married women declines and that as the age of children rises, the labor-force participation rate of married women rises.

Unequal Pay

The International Labor Office Convention 100, insuring women "equal pay for work of equal value," has been ratified by almost every European country. Many countries have passed equal pay laws. The net effect of the convention and the laws has been virtually nil. In fact, the sex differential in take-home pay has widened in the important British engineering industry in recent years (22:65).

The basic problem is: what is "work of equal value"? Where men and women do the same work it is certainly possible to enforce equal pay, if the employer and the union so desire. Sex differentials in civil service pay, for example, have been successfully eliminated in many countries, but what about the firm in which all the women are salesclerks and the male salesclerks are graded as "management trainees"? Employers are under no obligation to carry out a job evaluation under the British Equal Pay Act; and even a job evaluation could be manipulated to come out with the desired result, for example, by weighting heavily availability for heavy work, night work, or overtime. Women are prohibited from doing night work in most countries and generally try to avoid overtime because of family responsibilities.

The usual situation, however, in the occupations employing most women workers is that men and women do not do the same work; they are actually in different jobs. This situation is more difficult to resolve than the salesclerk-management trainee problem.

Another discouraging aspect of the situation, which practically guarantees that serious efforts to equalize pay in practice will not be made on any large scale in the near future, is the attitudes of the workers themselves, both men and women. Equal pay is not popular with males in the countries where unequal pay has the sanction of tradition; in England, according to *The Sunday Times,* "equal pay is as unpopular on the male-dominated shop floor as it is in the male-dominated boardroom" (22:65). Women, on the other hand, have been either uninterested or apathetic. Because women are rarely active in unions, even when they are members, unions often reflect the attitudes of their male members; they fail to press for the elimination of sex differentials in union contracts and the enforcement of equal pay laws as vigorously as they pursue pay raises.

CHAPTER 3   GREAT BRITAIN

The situation of women in the labor market in Great Britain is very similar to that in most countries and not quite so good as in the best countries. There is, however, a slight but distinctive nuance in the British scene, a nuance too slight to emerge from the statistical data, which all point to the average condition. Nevertheless, the interested observer can detect clues of the apparent extension to talented women determined to have careers of the well-known British tolerance of idiosyncrasy.

It is hard to document this observation. A reader of *The Times Literary Supplement* might easily gain the impression over the years that more women write nonfiction books in the United Kingdom than they do elsewhere. (Novelists and poets typically include women practitioners in most countries; nonfiction books are clearly less "feminine.") One gets the impression that there has been and continues to be a slightly higher proportion than elsewhere of determined girls who have broken out of the traditional mold and gone off to explore in Asia or dig in Greece or write a biography of some obscure historical figure. At present there are also more women in active politics than in the United States, although the absolute number is small.

The proportion of women in universities is not high either, although the aggregative data may be misleading. For example, in the United States the proportion of women faculty is higher than in Great Britain but most of them, until very recently, have been found in the traditional women's fields: education, home economics, and social work. In fact, there appear to be more eminent women professors in the traditional disciplines in England than elsewhere.

Labor-Force Participation Rates

British activity rates for women were very much like those for the United States (see Table 1). Women accounted for 36 percent of the total labor force in 1969; this percentage is a few points lower than the American ratio, but the other statistics were very close. The proportion of women fifteen years and older in the British labor force was 42 percent, the proportion of married women in the labor force amounted to 39 percent, and 60 percent of all women workers were married. Thirty-four percent of women with children worked in 1966 (17:70); the comparable figure for the United States in 1970 was 39 percent (78). Of the working mothers, one-fifth had at least one child under four years and almost half had a child five to eleven years old. All these figures represented substantial increases over the prewar period.

Occupational Distribution

The expansion in female employment after the war occurred largely in sectors with which women are traditionally associated, rather than through their entering fields that were mainly men's preserves. Occupations showing the greatest growth in the number of women employed were clerical work, teaching, nursing, social work, librarianship, and laboratory technician work. Within industry, the unskilled category showed the largest increase. The number of women journalists increased, as well as that of doctors and dentists; but the proportion of women in the professions as a whole rose only slightly, according to official sources, from 6 percent in 1921 to 8 percent in 1961 (87:362).

The labor market in the United Kingdom is segregated along the usual lines. Jobs tend to be advertised in newspapers as "Appointments" and "Women's Appointments," the latter largely devoted to requests for secretaries, personal assistants, and receptionists (5:21). In the main, women are heavily concentrated in the lower-level jobs in the service trades (40 percent of working women are in this sector), manufacturing (30 percent), and trade (20 percent).

Professions. The proportion of women in the professions is low and has not improved substantially over time. Medicine, with women constituting 18 percent of all doctors, was outstanding. Most of the choices open to girls center on teaching, nursing, or social work (49:555).

Prejudice is certainly part of the story. Two-thirds of the law chambers in England and Wales were reported to be closed to women; the floor of the London Stock Exchange was still, in 1971, barred to women; women who marry are usually dismissed from the foreign service—until 1961, they were required to retire (5:21; 51:13; 6:17).

Nevertheless, there were *some* women in all fields; they included actuaries, chartered accountants, and chemical, civil, mechanical, and electrical engineers (51:7). There were even 200 female company directors who had won the position by promotion, apart from those who had gained it by marriage or inheritance (15:60). Little discrimination was found in teaching, civil service, and, to some extent, local government service (7:75-77). In at least one profession, insurance, there seem to be some women at the top, and there is an expressed desire on the part of the professional association to recruit more women. The Chartered Insurers' Institute, with one percent of its membership female, expressed dissatisfaction with its failure to attract women; women were viewed as quite as suitable as men; and, in fact, several women had been elected local presidents—by men (31:189).

In 1961 a study was done of the employment experiences of two groups of Cambridge University graduates (7). The younger group, including both men and women, was then in their early thirties; the older group of women graduates, in their midforties. At graduation, a higher proportion of the women than of the men had received high honors. It is instructive to compare in Table 9 the types of jobs held by those who were working in 1961 (99 percent of the men, 51 percent of the younger women, 66 percent of the older women). The outstanding differences in Table 9 are in the proportions of each sex employed in industry and commerce —almost one-third of the men, very few of the women—and in teaching, where one-quarter of the men were to be found but 45 to 59 percent of the women. It is interesting to note, however, that the range of occupations was wider for the younger women than for the older graduates.

As one would expect, the distribution of earnings between men and women graduates was very skewed (see Table 10). In the work force as a whole, with two men for every woman working, men had the advantage among those earning £ 2,000 to 3,000 of 20 to 1 and at levels over £ 5,000 of 50 to 1 (15:3).

Medicine. Medicine is the British profession with the highest proportion of women, 18 percent in 1966. In fact, it has been included among the traditional careers for women (15:60). Nevertheless, very few of the medical specialists, the highly paid Harley Street consultants, are women.

Table 9: Employment of Cambridge University Graduates in 1961

	Men	Women	
	(1952-1953 Graduates)	(1952-1953 Graduates)	(1937-1938 Graduates)
Industry, commerce	32	6	1
Medicine	8	11	8
Other professions	11	2	5
Teaching			
Schools	14	24	44
Universities and technical			
colleges	10	21	15
Government service	11	10	11
Other	14	26	16
Total			
Percent	100	100	100
Number	2,611	148	131

Source: Christine Craig, *The Employment of Cambridge Graduates* (Cambridge: Cambridge University Press, 1963), p. 17.

Table 10: Earnings of Cambridge University Graduates in 1961

Earnings	Men (1952-1953 Graduates)	Women (1952-1953 Graduates)	Women (1937-1938 Graduates)
Under £ 1,250	24	66	34
£ 1,250-2,000	51	30	47
£ 2,000 and over	25	4	19
Total			
Percent	100	100	100
Number	2,611	148	131

Source: Christine Craig, *The Employment of Cambridge Graduates* (Cambridge: Cambridge University Press, 1963), pp. 31-33.

Women applicants are not judged by medical schools on the basis of merit alone. Discrimination in admission policies came under official scrutiny some years ago, and this study resulted in the University Grants Committee's setting 15 percent as the required minimum quota for women. The minimum has actually tended to become the maximum (49:555).

The women listed in the medical directory from 1960 to 1962 were surveyed in connection with a royal commission investigation of medical education. Almost half the respondents—there were 8,209 answers to a mailing of 11,594 names —were working full time at their profession; about one-third, part time; and 19 percent were not working. Slightly over half of those not working had children; but almost one-fifth of those not working, while married, had no children. Most of these women stated that they would like part-time employment but could find none available. Such a statistic, unfortunately, must have seemed to the admissions officers in medical schools to confirm their discriminatory entrance policy. The expensive investment necessary to produce doctors had a high waste component for women in that year in Great Britain (see Table 11).

Universities. In academic life, according to the secretary of the British Federation of University Women, promotion is very much slower for women: "If a man and woman both

Table 11: Employment of Women Medical Doctors in Great Britain, 1962

	Employed		
Marital status	Full time	Part-time	Not working
Single	81.7	12.6	5.7
Married:			
No children	54.4	28.8	16.8
Children up to five years	17.3	46.1	36.6
Children five years and over	30.1	50.5	19.4
Widowed, divorced	62.4	29.7	7.9
Total	47.1	34.2	18.7

Source: M. Jefferys and P. M. Elliott, *Women in Medicine* (London: Office of Health Economics, 1966), p. 13.

tried for the same post, the man would get the job. If you assess the prospects of a man and a woman with equal qualifications, it could take the woman 10 years to get as far as the man could get in five'' (50:11).

As of December 31, 1968, the ranks of women teaching and doing research in universities in the United Kingdom were as follows (74: Table 38):

	Total	Number of women	Percent of total
Professors	3,199	46	1.4
Readers and senior lecturers	5,554	369	6.6
Lecturers	16,648	1,624	9.8
Assistant lecturers and others	6,075	1,353	22.3

Ten of the women professors were in social studies; 19, in languages, literature, and the arts.

It is interesting that the distribution of faculty by rank remains very much the same in the new universities—all founded after World War II—as in the old. A comparison between data for 1961 and 1969 indicated that women had made no progress; in fact, the proportion in senior positions fell slightly.

The distribution of women faculty among fields was very uneven. Only 2 percent of the faculty in engineering and other applied sciences were women; 7 percent in pure science; 14 percent in social sciences; 15 percent in medicine, dentistry, and health; and 17 percent in the humanities.

Law. Women lawyers constitute 5 percent of all lawyers in Great Britain, a figure which, though low, is 66 percent greater than the comparable figure for the United States. Most of the women lawyers are solicitors rather than barristers (trial lawyers), the more glamorous, higher-paid part of the profession. Two-thirds of the firms in England and Wales were reported to be closed to women altogether (5:21).

Civil Service. ". . . Civil Service has travelled the road to complete equality in a resistant, hesitant manner" (14:237). Forced retirement at marriage was dropped in 1946; equal pay for the same work was not achieved until 1962. Pregnancy leaves of at least two months are now available to women.

The proportion of women falls as rank rises. Most of the women are clerical workers, a group which is half female. The top administrative class includes 220 women, 8.5 percent of the total number of administrators. The proportion of females among new entrants fell from 12 percent in the years 1948 to 1951 to 8 percent during 1952 to 1963, but rose to 18 percent in 1964 to 1967.

An interesting difference between men and women emerged from a study of the top administrative class: a majority of the women were unmarried. In 1966, 80 percent of the men were married, compared with only 35 percent of the women (14:316). Home responsibilities were thought by many of the respondents to constitute the "edge" required to get to the top, which gave men the advantage in the office. Married women reported that they felt tension and strain because of the competing demands on their time. This was particularly true of married women with children.

Politics. In 1967 the twenty-six women members of Parliament constituted 4.1 percent of the total membership. More of them were Labor than Conservative—5.5 percent of the Labor members, 2.8 percent of the Conservative (51:13). Both the Heath cabinet in 1972 and the shadow Labor cabinet included a woman in a prominent post.

School Teaching. Three-quarters of elementary school teachers and 46 percent of secondary school teachers are women, but few school heads are women, even in girls' schools. Moreover, there are few female applicants for these jobs. In Wales and the North, there is still prejudice against married women working and "taking jobs away from men," stemming from the 1930s (49:557).

Engineering. Engineering is a man's field. Some engineering firms will not employ women, and some branches of the industry are virtually barred to women. Because of the generally discouraging atmosphere in the industry, women do not exploit even those opportunities open to them: there were said to be more jobs open to women than applicants to fill them. The newest fields offered the greatest opportunities: electrical engineering, including computer work, and chemical engineering. Mechanical and civil engineering were considered less hospitable to women (49:561).

Professional associations in these fields reported the following percentages of female members in the mid-1960s (51:7):

Professional associations	*Female members*
Chemical engineering	0.02
Civil engineering	0.06
Electrical engineering	0.20
Mechanical engineering	0.07

Education and Training

Women constituted 30 percent of the university enrollment

in the United Kingdom¹ in 1968. There were sharp differences in the fields of major interest of women and men, as shown in Table 12.

Table 12:   Major Fields of University Students by Sex, 1968
(in percent)

	Men	Women
Science	27	23
Engineering and technology	23	1
Social administration and business studies	20	24
Language, literature, and area studies	8	26
Arts	6	13
Other	16	13
	—	—
Total	100	100

Source: University Grants Committee, *Statistics of Education: Universities, 1968-1969:* vol. 6 (London: HMSO, 1970), pp. 2-3.

Engineering and technology were much more popular among the men than among the women. Literature, on the other hand, was predominantly a female subject. Almost half the women graduates, 41 percent in 1969, took jobs connected with the arts, mainly teaching (73:5).

The distribution of majors in universities was foreshadowed by the differences in the curricula for boys and for girls at the secondary school level. A 1961 study revealed that the amount spent per pupil studying science in government schools was 13s.6d. for boys compared with 11s.6d. for girls. In the private schools, the spending rate for boys was 27s.2d. compared with only 12s. for girls. The interesting point here is not so much that local governments spent 16 percent more on the boys but that upper-class parents were even less interested in securing for their daughters as good a scientific education as for their sons (48:115).

Vocational training beyond the statutory school years is more popular with boys than with girls. Two-and-a-half times

¹The United Kingdom, of course, includes Northern Ireland in addition to Great Britain (England, Scotland, and Wales). The percentages were almost identical for Great Britain and the United Kingdom.

as many boys as girls have gone into jobs offering at least twelve months' training. Apprentices, for example, are over-whelmingly male. In 1964 of those leaving school before the age of eighteen, 36 percent of the boys but only 6 percent of the girls became apprentices in skilled trades (51:6). The girls concentrated in the traditionally feminine industries: in May 1967, in factories of ten or more workers, women held 27 percent of the apprenticeships in the clothing industry and 14 percent in textiles, but in all other industries they con-stituted less than 10 percent of the apprentices (49:578). The proportion of skilled women in industry has been falling because of the decline of the textile industry, which employed almost three-quarters of all the skilled women in 1911.

Equal Pay

An Equal Pay Act was passed in 1970, with 1975 set as the date by which equalization must be achieved. Progress has been very slow: in eighty-five wage settlements agreed to in 1970 by unions and employers, fourteen retained the sex differential unchanged; the average improvement in women's rates in the remaining settlements narrowed the gap only 2.5 percentage points. In twenty of these settlements, women's rates were less than 80 percent of men's, the lowest being only 57 percent.[2]

An estimate made in 1969 put the proportion of women receiving equal rates for equal work at only 10 percent; these included mainly workers in the civil service, local government, and the professions (88). Equal pay for clerical workers in the public service has been observed to have affected the sex differential in private employment in inner London and Edinburgh, but not elsewhere (49:566).

According to Routh, average hourly earnings of women in seven occupational classes amounted to 54 percent of men's just before World War I—and were still at that level in 1960. Women did work somewhat shorter hours, even when they worked full time. In October 1968 women manual workers

[2]*The Sunday Times* [London], February 28, 1971, p. 52.

averaged 70.4 cents an hour for a 38.2-hour week, while men earned $1.39 an hour for a 45.8-hour week, a differential of 51 percent. The comparable figure for full-time nonmanual workers in manufacturing was 53 percent and in all industries and services it was 60 percent (54:86).

Attitudes

Working Mothers. In a survey of over 7,000 women made in 1967 for the Ministry of Labor, almost half of the married women were working (43 percent of them less than 30 hours a week); three-quarters of those working were running a home in addition to holding a job; about two-thirds of them had children under sixteen. The percentage of mothers working by the age of a child in the home was as follows (25:29):

Age of child	Percent of mothers working
Two or under	15
3-4 years	21
5-15 years	44

Almost two-thirds of the mothers were working part time. Nevertheless, there was a strong feeling on the part of the women in the sample that women with children should not work (25:188).

Job Satisfaction. The same survey revealed interesting feelings about jobs among the women in the sample. Very few of them had senior jobs of any kind, and few had received any on-the-job training. Two-thirds of the sample were nonmanual workers—clerks, typists, salesclerks. Over half the manual workers were unskilled or semiskilled. Nevertheless, 55 percent of the working women reported that they were very satisfied with their jobs, and another 37 percent were fairly satisfied. The principal reason given for working was money, but two-thirds of those mentioning money also named another important reason for working; among these reasons, the one most frequently listed was the desire to have company and to escape boredom (19). Among the highly educated women, the boredom motive and the satisfaction of doing a job outweighed financial considerations.

A survey of 2,630 men and 494 women graduates of Cambridge University made a similar finding: among those employed, the women more often expressed satisfaction with their jobs, and less often dissatisfaction, than did the male respondents. The women were, as one would expect, earning substantially lower incomes than the men (see above, p. 36).

The greater satisfaction of women with jobs that are inferior in status and pay to men's was found in another survey. A study of women in the top administrative class of the civil service (14) revealed that, in the opinion of the women, the major difference between them and their male colleagues lay in ambition, drive, the desire to get ahead. More of the men wanted jobs with greater responsibility; the women did not want to be "dragons," as one woman put it (14:278). Interestingly, the women were not discontented because they were less successful than the men (there were five women in the highest 211 jobs; none was at the very top). On the contrary, they considered that they had succeeded quite well for women; they had the flattering impression that they were regarded as exceptional women for having achieved as much as they had (14:278). Furthermore, one-third of the women agreed with over half the men that women were less capable of holding top jobs.

An earlier study had also suggested that women did not aim for the top jobs, just for jobs with some responsibility. Even among the women reported to be capable of more responsible work by their supervisor, half did not want more responsible jobs (15:61).

Day Care

Among the working mothers with preschool children in the official survey made by Hunt, over 70 percent paid nothing for child care. About two-thirds listed a husband or other relatives as taking care of the children while they worked; most of them, it will be recalled, worked only part time. About 6 percent of the children under two years of age were in day nurseries, and about 12 percent of the three- and four-year-olds were in nursery schools (25:87).

CHAPTER 4 SCANDINAVIA

The four Scandinavian countries—Norway, Denmark, Finland, and Sweden—are among the most progressive in the world, with democratic governments, advanced social services, strong socialist parties and union movements, well-educated populations, and relatively high incomes. Sweden is the richest country in Europe, with a per capita gross national product that is three-fourths of the American level.

Scandinavians will claim that their women enjoy complete equality. Indeed, there is a tradition of matriarchy in eastern Finland, where the men used to be away for long periods hunting, fishing, or trading. The position of women within the family in all four countries is undoubtedly strong. It is significant that Scandinavian Airlines was the first to hire a woman pilot for international flights. Nevertheless, the labor market is segregated by sex very much as it is in other countries, and schooling also follows the familiar pattern of sexual divisions.

Although Americans tend to think of the Scandinavian countries as homogeneous, there are many subtle and a few great differences among them, as the visitor quickly learns from the Scandinavians themselves. One of the principal differences is in the sphere of women's employment: Norway has one of the lowest labor-force participation rates for women, almost as low as the Netherlands; whereas Finland and Sweden, on the other hand, have the highest in the West.

It is interesting to speculate on the reasons for Norway's divergence from the Scandinavian norm, but there are no obvious answers, from either economists or sociologists (see 20, 21, 24).

NORWAY

Labor-Force Participation Rates

Norway, along with Holland, is the exceptional case: very advanced by most standards, both are countries in which relatively few married women work. One is told in Norway that this is the result of the dispersal of population in a vast country, with many one-industry towns that provide jobs for the men in forestry and fishing but not for women. The same scattered population, however, is also found in Finland where a very high proportion of women work. The 1960 census figures for Norway indicate that, although there is variation between rural and urban areas, the labor-force participation rates of married women are low even in the urban areas: the figure for rural areas is 6.5 percent and for urban 15.7 percent. While 21 percent of the married women in Oslo, the largest city, were working in 1960, the comparable figure for Stockholm was 37 percent and for Helsinki 53 percent (24:389).

The demand for labor has been high in Norway since the end of World War II. Full employment has prevailed over the entire period, with great shortages in the traditional women's occupations—teaching, nursing, social work, child care. Nevertheless, there has been a steady *decrease* in the proportion of women in the labor force, from 27 percent in 1930 to 23 percent in 1960 (48:362). The explanation is probably that more women were getting married, the median age at marriage was going down, and the agricultural sector, which accounted for almost half the working women in 1875, was undergoing continuous shrinkage.

The emergence of the second peak, the employment of middle-aged women, had, nevertheless, become apparent by 1968 in a sample study of married women in the labor force (42:22). As in other countries, part-time employment was common: 40 percent of the married women in a government survey were employed part time.

A large sample survey conducted by the Central Statistical Bureau indicated that married women who were not working did not, on the whole, think that they would have any difficulty in finding jobs (42:35). Realistically, those in the cities were more optimistic than those in the small towns, although even in the latter 35 percent of the women stated that they could obtain work locally. The principal reason given for not working was children: over half the mothers believed that they were needed at home; another 10 percent cited the impossibility of making alternative provision for child care (42:36-37). Among unemployed women with no children under fifteen years, 30 percent stated that they would have too much work to do, too heavy a workload, if they went out to work[1] and another 25 percent cited poor health (42:39-40). Almost 40 percent of them characterized their husband's attitude toward their working as negative.

Occupational Distribution

Women workers were concentrated in relatively few occupations, the traditional women's work: in 1960 nearly half of them were in services, nearly one-fourth in offices and shops. The largest number, almost one-fifth of the total, were in domestic service. The industrial workers were mainly in the textile, clothing, and food industries.

Professions. There were few women in professional or technical fields in Norway. In 1960 women doctors made up 10 percent of the total and only one percent of the medical directors. Of 1,766 upper-level civil servants, 253 were

[1]Ownership of appliances among the women in the study throws some light on the burden of housework. The percentages were: refrigerator, 85 percent; vacuum cleaner, 87 percent; nonautomatic washer, 54 percent; automatic washer, 31 percent; dishwasher, 3 percent.

Women and Work

Table 13:   Industrial Distribution of Women Workers in Norway

Occupation	Percent
All women workers	100.0
Agriculture	3.9
Manufacturing	16.5
Nursing	6.3
Teaching	4.3
Clerical work	18.2
Sales	14.6
Domestic service	18.8
Other	17.4

Source: Norway, *Population Census 1960,* vol. III, table 11.

women. Despite a startling reference in an English source to women constituting one out of ten engineers in Norway (51:13), the actual number of women engineers in the 1960 census was 51 out of 8,977 or 0.6 percent. In teaching there was the usual hierarchy: 54 percent of elementary school teachers were women, but only one-quarter at the secondary level were women. With 9 percent women at the university level, there were only five women professors out of a total of 291, or less than 2 percent.

Education and Training

The comparatively low labor-force participation rate of married women and the concentration of those who do work in "women's occupations" are both foreshadowed in the education and training figures. In Norway, as elsewhere, the more educated the women, the higher their labor-force participation rates. This trend was particularly true among married women (24:389). The enrollment of women in universities, which has increased in the last decade, was still only 28 percent of the total in 1970. Among new students one-third were women; but the dropout rate for women has always been higher than for men, and less than 20 percent of the degrees were won by women (46:40). In 1969 only 3.6 percent of doctoral degrees were awarded to women. At the gymnasium (secondary school) level, there was less difference: in 1969 female graduates constituted just under 20 percent of the appropriate population in the country as a whole, and male graduates 24 percent (45:31).

The fields of major interest at universities showed the usual differences between men and women. For 1969 the figures were as follows:

| Major field | Percent | |
	Men	Women
Science	61	21
Arts	26	70
Commercial	13	9
Total	100	100

Philology (languages) was the most popular arts subject among girls. Pharmacology is the only unexpected note in women's fields: 92 percent of the degrees granted in 1970 were to women.

The disparity between the sexes is greater in vocational training courses than in the academic stream. "Today, as fifty years ago," a woman trade unionist stated, "women are brought up to prepare themselves for the role of housewife." Another writer pointed out that "For girls who have consciously or unconsciously accepted their future roles as housewives, a long and expensive vocational education would often seem wasted" (57:46). Thus, there were many more women in short courses in commercial subjects (typing, shorthand), in social work and health services schools—where they represented 94 percent of the total students in a recent year—and in teacher-training colleges. Technical schools, however, enrolled men almost exclusively. At the Institute of Technology, the 4.7 percent women in a student body of 3,000 in 1967 studied, in the main, architecture or chemistry (57:45). At craft and industrial schools, women went almost exclusively into dressmaking, hairdressing, housework, and cooking.

Equal Pay

Sex differentials were eliminated from collective agreements in the years 1961 to 1967. Nevertheless, women's average hourly earnings in manufacturing were only 74 percent of men's earnings in 1969; in clerical occupations, 92 percent; and for sales clerks, 76 percent.

Women made up a substantial proportion of the low-wage workers in 1965, those earning below 15,000 *kroner* a year, as can be seen below (80:387):

	Low-wage workers	
	Men	Women
	(percent)	
Manufacturing		
Wage earners	12	80
Salaried employees	3	43
Retail trade	18	67

A careful investigation in 1969 of the banking industry, which classified employees by education and age to eliminate the influence of these factors on earnings differentials between men and women, revealed an imbalance of the sexes in top jobs. A similar study of local government employees yielded the same results (57:70).

Nevertheless, equal pay is not regarded as an urgent issue and is not accorded high priority in Norway, even by the women themselves (80:392).

Provision for Child Care

There is very little communal provision for the care of pre-school children in Norway. Less than 9,000 places were available in 1965, about one-fifth the number in Denmark, and 12,000 in 1969, and this lack is a significant obstacle to employment outside the home of mothers with young children. Not only is day care for young children inadequate, but the school starting age is late—seven years—and thereafter, until fifth or sixth grade, classes in many schools are held for different hours each day but for less than a full day (57:64). In these circumstances the dovetailing of school hours with even part-time employment would be extremely difficult.

Attitudes

A recent government survey of married women (42) revealed that even a substantial proportion, 38 percent, of those actually working opposed, in principle, the taking of employment outside the home by married women. A majority, 57 percent, of the married women not working disapproved. Husbands were reported by their wives to divide the same way, but more strongly: 47 percent of the husbands with working wives and 70 percent of the husbands with nonworking wives were reported to disapprove of married women working.

The results suggest that the traditional role of women is widely accepted in Norway.

A study of parents' attitudes on education supports this finding:

. . . most Norwegians now subscribe to the ideology of equality between the sexes, and maintain that boys and girls should receive the same upbringing and education. But recent research into public attitudes in this field indicates that this ideology is superficial and does not correspond to deeper attitudes and feelings or to actual behavior. In one study, about 75 mothers in the city of Oslo, who had children in the second or fifth grades, were chosen at random to be interviewed. Over 95 percent of them answered *yes* to the question, "Do you think that boys and girls should be brought up as far as possible alike?" when the mothers were questioned more specifically about actual treatment of children, however, their agreement was significantly less. Asked whether boys and girls should help equally with household chores, 77 percent replied *yes*, but 23 percent had clear reservations or answered *no*. To the question, "Do you think boys or girls should have the best education?" barely half answered that they thought both sexes should have the same. The rest would give boys the advantage, at least if they had to make a choice. No one thought that girls ought to have a better education than the boys (57:46-47).

Politics

There are outstanding women in politics in Norway; but, in percentage terms, the number of participants is not unusually large. Women constituted 9 percent of the members of the *Storting* in a recent year, compared with 4 percent in Great Britain's Parliament and 17 percent in Finland's legislature.

In local government elections in the fall of 1971, the representation of women in all parties doubled or tripled in ten councils, giving women the majority for the first time in three cities, including Oslo and Trondheim. The results on a national scale were not great—the number of women rose from 9.5 percent in 1967 to 15 percent out of a total of about 13,500 representatives, but the impact on the ten councils affected was dramatic. The explanation for what was called a "coup" gradually emerged from newspaper accounts. The proportional representation system used in Norwegian municipal elections permits the listing of a candidate's name twice. The printed ballots distributed by each of the political parties make use of this provision, listing their top candidates—the most distinguished senior party members—twice in succession in order to increase their chances of election. Normally the women are clustered at the bottom of the list, the riskier part as far as election is concerned. Because the overwhelming majority of Norwegians vote a straight ticket, it is possible —a book pointed out this possibility in 1967—for a small number of people to alter the order of listing. A small group, possibly the new feminists—the secret has been well kept— apparently organized enough write-in votes in 1971 to elect many more women than ever before; on any one of the party ballots, the conspirators crossed out the names of men at the top of the slate and substituted women from other party lists. As a result, the woman who was number thirty-five and thirty-six on the Labor party list, for example, ended up with more votes than the incumbent mayor, who was number one and two on the Labor party slate. The same thing happened with other parties' candidates. This clever, conspiratorial manipulation of the electoral process aroused controversy; but Norway was certainly jolted, and the participation of women in local government rose dramatically.

DENMARK

Denmark has been the pioneer, along with Sweden, in many areas of social policy: for example, the repeal of all legal restrictions on pornography and legislation to protect illegitimate children, in addition to its early enactment of social insurance, public housing, and other elements of the welfare state. One would expect to find here, surely, that women are more nearly equal than elsewhere; in fact, they are not. A brief description of the labor market reveals many of the familiar characteristics prevailing in the other countries surveyed.

Labor-Force Participation Rates

In the last decade the employment picture has changed markedly for women. From 30 percent of the total labor force in 1960, the proportion of women rose to 38 percent by 1969. The increase came largely from married women, who made up 40 percent of the working women in 1960 and 60 percent in 1969.

Nevertheless, fewer than half the married women were in the labor force in 1969, a smaller proportion than in Finland or Sweden. Most married women continued to quit work at the birth of their first child. As the children grew older, some women returned to work—the younger women now in greater numbers than the older generations had at their age—and the fewer the children the more likely the mothers were to return to work. The second peak, composed of middle-aged women returning to the labor market, was just becoming visible in 1965. Similarly, the more education and training they had had the more likely married women were to return to work (9:142-50).

About half the married women worked part-time (less than thirty hours a week). A higher percentage, 71 percent of a large sample study, reported that they preferred part-time, but that there were not enough openings (9:150).

Occupational Distribution

Women were predominantly concentrated in unskilled work in industry, shops, offices, and service occupations. Some extension in the range of "women's jobs" has occurred recently, with openings for women in "the lower levels of computer work, as draughtswomen and laboratory assistants, and as taxi, bus and tram drivers" (54:44).

The older women in rural areas often worked in service occupations, particularly domestic work, while the younger women, and those in the urban areas, were more often employed in offices or as nurses or teachers. Less than half covered in a large survey had received any vocational training. The most prevalent types of vocational training were in nursing and teaching, with a substantial number receiving training in sewing and hairdressing (9:149).

The small family farm still persists in Denmark, and over half of the "Helping wives" in Table 14 are farmers' wives. Agriculture is declining in importance, and many of these women are coming onto the labor market.

University education had, in 1965, a ratio of one woman to two men. Almost half the women studied humanities; medicine accounted for almost one-quarter. Science and technology attracted only 11 percent of the women in 1965 and 1966. Among men, the humanities accounted for 17 percent; medical sciences, 20 percent; and science and technology, 30 percent.

Professions. According to Sullerot, one-quarter of the doctors in Denmark are women, and the proportion of women dentists is the same. Among lawyers, 10 percent are women. These are very high rates for the Western countries.

Table 14: Occupational Distribution of Employed Population,
Denmark, 1967

Occupation	Men Number	Men Percent	Women Number	Women Percent
Independent, in trade and professions	349,100	23.6	43,700	5.1
Public service and administration	404,800	27.4	383,600	44.5
Public administration, defense	28,400	1.9	1,400	.2
Teachers	33,000	2.2	36,700	4.3
Librarians, scientists, clergymen, etc.	5,900	.4	3,300	.4
Health service	9,400	.6	62,000	7.2
Railway and postal employees	44,500	3.0	2,800	.3
Banks	13,200	.9	8,500	1.0
Shipping	10,900	.7		
Telephone operators	200	.1	6,900	.8
Office employees	83,700	5.7	157,000	18.2
Shop assistants, commercial employees	77,900	5.3	77,700	9.0
Engineers, architects	28,400	1.9	600	.1
Other technical employees	53,300	3.6	18,000	2.1
Other	16,000	1.1	8,700	1.0
Skilled workers	305,100	20.6	15,100	1.7
Unskilled workers	419,300	28.4	262,700	30.5
Factory workers	120,900	8.2	85,700	9.9
Cleaning staff	1,700	.1	108,300	12.6
Other	296,700	20.1	68,700	8.0
Domestic workers			40,600	4.7
Helping wives			116,200	13.5
Total	1,478,300	100.0	861,900	100.0

Source: OECD, *Employment of Women* (Paris: OECD, 1970), pp. 288, 290.

Equal Pay

Equal pay for equal work is the rule in public service, and in some trades it is included in union agreements. Nevertheless, among unskilled workers, women's hourly earnings in the midsixties averaged only 82 percent of men's (48:293).

Sixty-two percent of the working women in the survey by the Danish National Institute of Social Research earned less than $1,360 in 1964, a low level of income for two reasons: about half worked part-time, and the women received lower rates than men for similar work (48:150).

SWEDEN

Not only is Sweden second to Finland in terms of the proportion of women workers, but the Swedish government is also outstanding in having formulated a radical policy to eliminate the "dual labor market," as part of a broader program to enforce equality between the sexes in every sphere. The policy of the government, however, should not be mistaken for current practice, as it has been by some Women's Liberation partisans in the United States.

Government policy has been based on the views of some intellectuals, which have been widely accepted at the official level. The Swedish people, particularly in the rural areas, are as resistant to change, however, as people in other countries, and Swedish realities do not correspond to the policy declarations made to United Nations committees (33:33). Tight labor-market conditions have facilitated the increased entry of women into some traditionally male occupations, such as engineering; but there are still two labor markets in Sweden, one for men and one for women.

Labor-Force Participation Rates

Of the Western countries, only Finland has higher indices of women in employment than Sweden. In 1970, 54 percent of all women from ages sixteen to seventy-four were employed; women made up 40 percent of the total labor force; the proportion of married women working was 53 percent; and 71 percent of the mothers of children from seven to sixteen years old were employed.

Part-time work was very common, however: half of the married women worked part-time. Regional imbalance was also characteristic of women's employment, as in Norway: in some areas dominated by mining or forestry less than 15 percent of married women could find work.

Occupational Distribution

Three-quarters of all employed women were in twenty-five occupations in which women made up over half the employees and in most cases substantially more than half. The proportion of men in these occupations was only 14 percent (see Table 15).

More than half the male workers were in mining, manufacturing, and construction, industries that accounted for only 20 percent of the employed women. The overall figures do not reveal the division that exists within broad categories between men's jobs and women's. Within the government sector, for example, women constituted 67 percent of all employees, but in the two top salary grades there were 5,908 men and 161 women (Table 16). Furthermore, 90 percent of of the women were in the bottom half of the various salary grades, compared with less than two-thirds of the men.

Equal Pay. In 1960 the Swedish Employers' Confederation and the Swedish Confederation of Trade Unions agreed to abolish lower wage rates for women within five years. Nevertheless, although lower rates are now rare, great differences in earnings exist. The average earnings of female industrial workers in November 1968, while an improvement over the 70 percent prevailing at the beginning of the 1960s, were still only 79 percent of men's.

Education and Training

Although girls now go to secondary schools as frequently as boys, they study different subjects. In 1968, for example, over one-quarter of the boys, but only 1 percent of the girls, opted for technical fields. More than a third of the girls, compared with only 6 percent of the boys, elected the humanities.

Table 15: Occupations in Which More Than 10,000 Women Were Employed in 1965

	Number of women	Percent of total employment
Shop assistant	127,898	79.5
Secretary, typist	74,592	95.6
Agricultural worker	62,351	54.5
Cleaner	57,346	90.8
Hospital attendant	56,381	98.5
Domestic servant, children's nurse	52,221	99.7
Specialized office worker	50,713	67.6
Office worker	36,422	81.7
Clothing worker	35,909	98.3
Accountant, office cashier	35,638	70.0
Waiter, barman	28,884	89.0
Form-master	27,980	74.8
Nurse	25,658	99.8
Kitchen help	24,904	95.0
Telephone operator	21,497	99.0
Retail dealer, shop manager	18,905	29.1
Hairdresser, beautician	17,728	73.5
Home help, etc.	17,578	100.0
Textile worker	14,352	55.3
Cook	13,960	82.5
Cattleman, etc.	13,206	73.0
Packer	12,603	65.6
Technical and laboratory assistant	11,517	56.7
Cashier, shop and restaurant	11,337	97.7
Housekeeper	10,583	77.3
Total	860,163	73.4

Source: National Labor Market Board of Sweden, *Women and the Labor Market*, p. 25.

The number of women entering universities was 42 percent of the total in 1965; but, with more women students dropping out, their proportion among graduates at the first level was 37 percent. For higher degrees, the number of women declined precipitously: they constituted 16 percent of the candidates for the second degree and only 8 percent for the doctorate (33:72).

Table 16: Swedish Civil Service Employees by Level, Grade, and Sex, 1966

Grade	Level A 1,000-4,000 kr.		Grade	Level B 4,200-5,700 kr.		Grade	Level C 5,800-10,000 kr.	
	Men	Women		Men	Women		Men	Women
	(Percent)							
1-9	10.7	58.2	1			1	2,138	42
10-14	52.6	31.6	2	1		2	459	4
15-19	21.2	6.6	3	105	12	3	148	2
20-24	9.8	2.9	4	2		4	99	
25-29	5.7	0.7	5	2,467	94	5	71	1
			6	308	6	6	91	
Total	100.0	100.0						
			7	7		7	2	
						8	10	
Total Number	141,855	84,628		2,890	112		3,018	49

Source: *Sweden Today: The Status of Women in Sweden: Report to the United Nations 1968* (Stockholm: The Swedish Institute), p. 92.

At the universities, as in the lower schools, sex divisions in fields of study existed: in 1965, 46 percent of the women studied humanities, and 12 percent science and technology subjects; for men, on the other hand, the most popular field was science and technology (36 percent), with only 16 percent in the humanities.

Vocational training also divided along traditional lines. Ninety percent of the girls taking courses in 1965 studied for one year only; 85 percent of them took office work, household work, nursing and sales courses. Half the boys took longer courses—two years or more; and most of those chose industrial, handicraft, or technical education.

Day Care

There are about 50,000 places for the children of working parents in day nurseries and private families supervised by the local authorities, but these are quite inadequate to meet the demand. According to an inquiry made in 1966, there were 317,000 children under ten whose mothers worked more than fifteen hours a week, and another 150,000 below school age (70:13).

Government Policy on Sex Roles

We referred at the beginning of this section to a radical policy adopted by the Swedish government and aimed at eliminating the differentiation of sex roles. Nothing less, it was held, would ensure complete equality for women in fact as well as in law. Several years of lively debate on women's rights, in the press, on television, and in organizations ended with the broadening of the question to the more fundamental area of sex roles in the home. As a government report to the United Nations developed this theme (72:4-6):

A decisive and ultimately durable improvement in the status of women cannot be attained by special measures aimed at women alone; it is equally necessary to abolish the conditions which tend to assign certain privileges, obligations or rights to men. No decisive change in the distribution of functions and status as between the sexes can be achieved if the duties of the male in society are assumed *a priori* to be unaltered. . . . The division of functions as between the sexes must be changed in such a way that both the man and the woman in a family are afforded the same practical opportunities of participating in both active parenthood and gainful employment. . . .

* * * * *

. . . . Eventually to achieve complete equality . . . , a radical change in deep-rooted traditions and attitudes must be brought about among both women and men, and active steps must be taken by the community to encourage a change in the roles played by both. The view that women ought to be economically supported by marriage . . . is a direct obstacle to the economic independence of women and their ability to compete on equal terms in the labor market. Similarly, the husband's traditional obligation to support his wife must be modified to constitute a responsibility, shared with her, for the support of the children. . . .
The Government is well aware that this view appears revolutionary and unrealistic in the eyes of the represent-

atives of many other countries. A growing opinion in Sweden has however rallied to its support. In Sweden, as in the other Scandinavian countries, a lively debate has been going on . . . concerning the tasks of men and women in society and the home. This debate has brought forth a new approach which involves a departure from the traditional habit of regarding these problems as "women's questions."

The debate has received great support from scientific research concerning the roles of the sexes; the research has been conducted mainly by sociologists. . . . The analyses . . . show that no rapid advancement of women in employment and in the professions, politics, trade union activity, etc., is possible as long as men fail to assume that share of the work of the home that falls to them as husbands and fathers. The expression "male emancipation" has therefore been coined in Sweden to denote the right of a husband to remain at home while the children are small where it is found more appropriate for the mother to devote herself to gainful employment. The demand for male "emancipation" in family life is also supported by the results of recent psychological research, which have proved that the identification of growing boys may become uncertain in a one-sided, mother-dominated home environment.[1] This lack of certainty in identification (of what is 'manly' behavior) may lead to overcompensation expressed in exaggerated aggressiveness and may be one explanation of the higher crime rate as compared to girls. In recent years demands have been made for a change in legislation whereby the father, like the mother (when she interrupts her career) would be entitled to a certain leave of absence with pay while the children are small. The need for male staff in child care institutions, day nurseries, nursery schools and the lower schools has been emphasized in many quarters.

[1]Per Olav Tiller, "Parental Role Division and the Child's Personality Development," in *The Changing Roles of Men and Women*, ed., Edmund Dahlstrom, pp. 79-104 (London: Gerald Duckworth and Co., Ltd. 1967).

Implementation of Policy. Measures that have been initiated include the encouragement of girls in undertaking more education and training in what are considered traditional men's fields; labor-market policies to procure more jobs for women; the expansion of child care facilities. A recent change has been made in elementary schools, on the reasoning that sex roles become fixed very early in life: in the nine-year comprehensive schools, both boys and girls are instructed in cooking and child care; and metal work, woodwork, and needlework, were made compulsory for all boys and girls in grades up to sixth by an act of parliament in 1968.

Textbooks are being examined with a view to expunging the familiar material supporting the traditional division of occupations; instead, there will be pictures of male nurses and women engineers (72:34).

Labor-Market Policy. Set up initially to pursue a unique "active labor-market policy" in a full employment situation, the Swedish Labor Market Board administers several programs, including training and retraining courses, transfer allowances, work relief ,vocational guidance, and the employment service. For reasons of equity as well, the board has been concerned with the problems of women workers and of women who would like to work if suitable work were available.

The labor supply in Sweden has been tight for decades, with reliance on temporary immigrant laborers from southern Italy and other Mediterranean countries. It was rational economic policy to induce married women to return to the labor market. Many individual companies experimented successfully with part-time female workers, hiring them for jobs that were traditionally handled by men.

The Labor Market Board has attempted to develop both the supply and demand for women workers. It has attempted to induce women to take part in the wide range of technical training it offers, and it has persuaded some employers to develop openings for women with shorter hours or flexible working arrangements. The number of women undertaking training for jobs not traditionally held by women was reported to be still small but, on the employment front, the Labor Market Board has had some outstanding successes (54:79-83).

1. Volvo, the automobile manufacturer, began to employ women on the assembly line in 1961 because of the shortage of labor. A group piecework system was in effect, and on the average women took one or two weeks to get up to bonus standard—one day longer, it was estimated, than men required. The women were introduced gradually, and the men's initial objections were gradually overcome. The women were judged to be less flexible than men and were not used on all jobs; but some were assigned to the "dirty" but high-paying jobs "under the chassis." Volvo reported that the women had higher absentee and accident rates, but lower overall wastage rates. Part-time arrangements had worked well—part-time workers were found to be more reliable. Women did not tend to be promoted to the more responsible jobs, but about 10 percent of middle-management posts in engineering, laboratories, sales, purchasing, and personnel were held by women.

2. Atlas Copco, manufacturer of rock drills and equipment for wagon drills for mining, surveyed all the jobs in the company with a view to employing more women and decided that as many as three-fourths of them were suitable for older women. The range of women's jobs has, therefore, expanded. Some women are working in the most skilled jobs, in which three years are required to reach full proficiency.

3. ASEA, manufacturer of equipment for power generation and transmission and electric motors and appliances, with 980 female employees out of a total of 5,000 workers, experimented with twenty-two part-time older women workers because of the difficulty of getting labor. All were given a training course, and six years later all twenty-two were still working for the company; many of them, at their own request, were full time. Women employees tend to take advantage of the shorter rather than the longer courses in the extensive training program run by the company, but a small number

have qualified as supervisors and engineers and some are training for highly skilled jobs such as pattern makers and electricians. Draughtswomen have also completely replaced draughtsmen.

4. In 1962 the shortage of postmen led the Gothenberg Post Office to experiment with the employment of postwomen. Middle-aged women were recruited. The postmen were initially doubtful that women could handle the job, but in fact the women were able to carry the entire load and perform all the tasks, with an absentee rate lower than the men's. The only adjustments made for the women were the designing of a special push cart and the cutting down of delivery districts.

Summary: Current Situation. Despite the lofty aims of government policy, it is worth repeating—and this will come as no surprise after the brief review of actual conditions in Sweden—that these goals are very far from accomplished. To quote the report to the United Nations on *The Status of Women:* "The efforts made up to now are still inadequate to offer any hope of practical equality between men and women for a long time to come" (72:27).

FINLAND

Labor-Force Participation Rates

Finland is often cited as the most egalitarian society in the West on the basis of two statistics: first, 50 percent of all university students are women; and, second, over half of all married women were working as early as 1960. These are, in their respective categories, the highest percentages in the West.

Some may also recall that Finnish women were, in 1906, the first in Europe to get the vote. Their 1965 representation in parliament, 17 percent, is also relatively high; the comparable figure for Norway, for example, was 9 percent, and for Great Britain, 4 percent.

Finland has a large agricultural sector in which 32 percent of the working women and 38 percent of the male workers are occupied. Finland is not, however, a backward country in which a high female labor-participation rate merely reflects the existence of a large agricultural sector, because the proportion of married women working is just as high in the towns as in the rural areas. The percentage in Helsinki in 1960 was 53, much higher than the 37 percent in Stockholm.

Occupational Distribution

The range of women's employment in Finland is wider than in other noncommunist countries. Visitors have been struck by the sight of women street cleaners and construction workers. The general picture, however, is not so different from the Western norm, as the following figures indicate:

	Percent of working women
Agriculture	31.6
Manufacturing	17.0
Clerical and sales work	27.6
Other	23.8
Total	100.0

Within manufacturing, more than half the women workers are in textiles, dressmaking, and food processing, a distribution which follows the typical Western pattern. Additional evidence is the following list of "women's occupations," in which women constitute at least half the working force and which account, in turn, for about one-third of all women workers.

Occupation	Women Number	Percent of total in occupation
Nurses	11,893	100.0
Cashiers in shops and restaurants	3,143	99.7
Beauticians, laundry and cleaning women, domestic workers	112,232	97.8

Occupation *Continued*	Women Number	Percent of total in occupation
Stenographers and typists	6,263	96.0
Cashiers in banks and offices	4,714	92.3
Bank clerks	7,960	88.5
Pharmacists	3,128	85.8
Bookkeepers	7,111	81.9
Librarians, museum officials	980	73.4
Mental care nurses	2,874	69.5
Elementary school teachers	14,405	63.1
Social workers	2,310	62.9
Sales persons	84,891	60.4

Source: Finland, *Census, 1960,* Table 2.

Professions. Among the professions, dentistry and pharmacy were predominantly female, with 77 percent and 86 percent of all practitioners. This is a Northern European phenomenon. The proportion of women doctors was about as high as anywhere in the West, 23.4 percent. There was also a relatively high proportion of women barristers and solicitors, 9.6 percent; and, even more surprisingly, 11 percent of the judges were women (12:Table 2). In addition, one-quarter of the architects were women. Very few women worked in the engineering professions, with the exception of "other" engineering occupations, probably drafting, which considerable numbers of women have entered in Sweden, Denmark, and the Federal Republic of Germany (54:14-15).

Education and Training

According to one writer, the factor that contributes the most to the limited participation of women in professional careers is the attitude of the women themselves. "They still consider marriage as the feminine career *par excellence,* and young girls pass their time dreaming of a good husband instead of studying in order to have a good profession" (1:9).

Sex differences were substantial in education. Girls make up 56 percent of the Finnish general secondary school students, where 62 percent of them opted for the language major; 64 percent of the boys chose mathematics. Boys attended, in greater numbers, the vocational secondary schools, where they studied technical subjects. Girls, on the other hand, studied commercial subjects, cooking and home-making, nursing, and dressmaking (1:10). At the universities, where women formed 51 percent of the student body, almost half of them majored in the humanities, which attracted only 11 percent of the men. In comparison with other countries, however, Finnish women did study mathematics and sciences in large numbers, as well as social sciences and medicine. Nevertheless, technology and engineering remained a male bailiwick, with only 7 percent women; and most of these were interested in architecture or textile technology.

Among the university students, women tended to drop out more than men, and they made up only 40 percent of the graduates in 1964. At the doctoral level, women numbered merely 12 percent in 1966 (1:12).

Child Care

There is no effective child care system in Finland (20:347). The percentage of working mothers who resorted to institutional child care has been put at only 2 percent (24:397).

Attitudes

In labor-market and educational indices, as we have seen, Finland excels. It is disappointing, then, to read the conclusion of a sociologist, who has made several studies, that there is a discrepancy between the formal participation of women in the economic, educational, and political life of the country and the general attitudes of the Finnish people (20:343). Attitudes on "women's role" appeared in fact to be more traditional among both Finnish men and women than among Swedes or Norwegians.

An interview survey of almost 1,000 women in Helsinki in 1966 revealed that, in 70 to 85 percent of the families, the wife alone prepared dinner, washed up, marketed, fed the children, cleaned house, made the beds, washed the dishes. Husbands participated frequently only in putting the children to bed and washing the windows. Husbands of working wives helped more (in 30 percent of the families) with these tasks than husbands of wives who stayed at home (15 percent). As a result, the total working day of the employed woman was on the average two hours longer than her husband's. Although the average earnings of women workers were only 60 percent of men's because of their doing lower-paid work—it is now illegal to pay lower rates for the same job—the women in the study were nevertheless more satisfied with their work and their lives, in general, than the men were. This satisfaction is an indication, according to the author, of their limited expectations and lower aspirations (10:126).

There is a long cultural tradition in the eastern part of the country of "matriarchy," because the men, in fishing, trading, and lumbering, customarily spent long periods away from home, leaving the women to mind the farm. Women are today more involved in local politics in eastern than in western Finland, but there are no significant differences in the home or in the rest of Scandinavia" (10:127).

Although in "some formal respects women in Finland are more independent and emancipated in their behavior than women in other Scandinavian countries," Haavio-Mannila concluded that "informal behavior and attitudes towards women's power in society and the family and towards division of the household tasks are more traditional in Finland than in the rest of Scandinavia" (10:127).

CHAPTER 5 FOUR OTHER WESTERN EUROPEAN COUNTRIES

FRANCE

Labor-Force Participation Rates

Because farmers' wives were automatically counted as employed, the contraction of the French agricultural sector, though it still remains substantial, meant a decline in the proportion of women in the labor force: from 37 percent in 1906 to 33 percent in 1962 (39:46). After 1962, the women's labor-force participation rate began to rise: from 1962 to 1968 very slightly, from 42.8 to 43.5 percent, for all women; a little more, from 40.5 to 43.1 percent, for women in nonagricultural households; and most of all for *married* women in the non-agricultural population, from 26.7 to 31.1 percent (53:181). During this period, the labor-force participation rate among men fell, because boys were staying in school longer, a factor which must also have kept the rate for women from rising even more than it did.

Activity rates among married women varied directly with the number of children under age seventeen: in 1962 among women under sixty years, 47.5 percent of those with no children were employed; 40.4 percent of those with one child; 26.1 percent of those with two children; and 16.5 percent of those with three children (48:312). The labor-force participation rate for all married women was 37.8 percent (54:55).

Women's economic activity rose with education—to a high of 80 percent for women with a university-level degree (48:301-2).

Salaire unique. Special allowances are paid by the government to married women who do not work, which probably operates to discourage the employment of women who would not earn much if they did work. In any event, the wives of unskilled workers are less likely to work than the wives of semiskilled or skilled workers, of clerical or middle-level executives (48:314).

Occupational Distribution

The largest proportion of women, one-third of the total, was in clerical occupations in 1968. These traditionally feminine occupations absorbed the greater part of the increase in working women: women rose as a percentage of all clerical workers from 53 percent in 1954 to 61 percent in 1968 (54:57). The unexpectedly high twelve percent of women in "middle-level executive" positions in 1968 (see Table 17) can be easily explained: nurses, social workers, and primary school teachers—occupations in which women were 60 to 80 percent of the total number of employees—were classified under this impressive title. Similarly, secondary and higher-school teachers accounted for almost half of the 3 percent of women in the "liberal professions and higher executives" category.

A striking figure in the French census points to a well-known French phenomenon, the female small-scale entrepreneur: half the "petits commerçants," subsumed under "Entrepreneur" in Table 17, were women.

Within the manual-worker category, there was a marked difference in the skill qualifications of the men and women. For example, for all manufacturing combined the percentages of skilled workers by sex in each of three categories were as follows (48:305):

Skill level	*Men*	*Women*
	Percent	
1 (low)	17.7	9.0
2 (medium)	14.0	3.0
3 (high)	9.0	1.2

Table 17: Socio-occupational Classification of Economically Active
Persons in France by Sex, 1968

Category	*Men* Number	Percent	*Women* Number	Percent
Farmers	1,527,780	11.5	932,060	13.1
Agricultural workers	527,200	4.0	61,000	.9
Entrepreneurs	1,276,940	9.6	685,040	9.6
Industrial	68,940	.5	10,220	.1
Craftsmen	532,340	4.0	90,460	1.3
Fishermen	16,380	.1	1,980	.0
Merchants	143,840	1.1	69,660	1.0
Shopkeepers	515,440	3.9	512,720	7.2
Liberal professions and higher executives	806,600	6.1	186,200	2.6
Professions	114,920	.9	27,600	.4
Teachers and others	114,700	.9	94,380	1.3
Administrators and engineers	576,980	4.3	64,220	.9
Middle-level executives	1,197,360	9.0	816,740	11.5
Primary school teachers and others	212,360	1.6	352,000	4.9
Medical and social services	28,600	.2	147,720	2.1
Technicians	474,120	3.6	59,820	.8
Administrators	482,280	3.6	257,200	3.6
Clerical workers	1,188,300	8.9	1,841,600	25.9
Manual workers	6,128,840	46.0	1,569,760	22.0
Service workers	245,200	1.8	925,860	13.0
Other	417,420	3.1	105,260	1.5
Total	13,315,640	100.0	7,123,520	100.0

Source: *Institut national de la statistique et des études économiques,
Economie et statistique,* 2 juin 1969, Table 3, p. 43.

Equal Pay

Net annual earnings of women employed in the private and semipublic sectors in 1966 amounted to 63 percent of men's earnings (86:17).

Education and Training

In the universities, women are concentrated in the humanities. Pharmacy is becoming a woman's field, as in some other European countries. It should be noted that law is a general subject in Europe, more similar to political science than to law school in the United States, and it does not prepare students for the practice of law.

Table 18:   Enrollment in French Universities by Field and Sex, 1960

	Men	Women	
	Number	Number	Percent of Total
Total	109,370	72,330	39.8
Law	20,720	8,675	29.5
Science	43,115	20,305	32.0
Humanities	21,670	31,025	58.9
Medicine	20,800	7,655	26.9
Pharmacy	3,065	4,670	60.4

Source: OECD, *Employment of Women* (Paris: OECD, 1970), p. 306.

Apprenticeship programs were, in the main, for boys. Almost three-and-a-half times as many boys as girls fifteen to nineteen years old were serving apprenticeships in 1962 (48:307). More boys than girls were attending technical and vocational schools. Almost all the girls learning an industrial trade were in dressmaking, a declining industry; about 60 percent of the boys, on the other hand, were studying mechanical, electrical, and radio engineering and electronics (48:308-9).

Day Care

In 1965 day nurseries could accommodate 19,700 children for the 6 million employed mothers. Provision for another 10,000 children was planned (48:316).

Nursery schools, *écoles maternelles,* enrolled two million children from three to six years old; at six French children start regular school. Fifty-two percent of all three-year-olds were accommodated in the nursery schools, over 80 percent of the four-year-olds, and 99 percent of the five-year-olds. These preschool programs are highly regarded; they are more than institutionalized baby-sitters, with educational activities designed to develop the children intellectually as well as in other ways (81:56). Because the children return home for the traditional two-hour lunch, however, nursery schools do not solve the problems of working mothers unless they work for only a few hours a day.

Cultural Patterns

The long lunch hour in France, when the main meal of the day is served, undoubtedly deters many women from working and makes life more difficult for those who do. In a subtler sense, this cultural pattern clearly influences the role of women: the relatively greater importance placed on food by the French, of which the long lunch hour is one manifestation, tends to make the housewife's role more important, and thus more satisfying to French women, than it is in our society, where achievement is highly esteemed and consumption relatively slighted. There is a significant difference in "life styles" between the French—and to some extent other Europeans as well—and Americans.

FEDERAL REPUBLIC OF GERMANY

Labor-Force Participation Rates

Although almost half the German women between fifteen and sixty-five years were working in 1961, and only 12 percent of them part-time, the overwhelming proportion of both men and women queried in a study of attitudes—75 percent and 72 percent—considered that this situation was not "normal" (61:20). Seventy percent of the women thought that a working woman should give up her job at the birth of her first child; as many as one-quarter believed that women should not work after marriage.

The demographic distribution underlying the labor-force figures indicated that the situation was indeed abnormal. Because of German war losses, there were more women than men in the over-forty age groups and, consequently, there is a high proportion of unmarried women. In the late 1960s women still accounted for 54 percent of the population over fifteen years of age. As Table 1 (p. 18) shows, the proportion of women in the total labor force, 37 percent, was not particularly high. The proportion of *married* women working, one-third, was also fairly low. The very high figure of 47 percent for the proportion of working women to all women fifteen to sixty-five years was attributable to the high proportion of *unmarried* women of whom almost three-quarters were in the labor force.

Occupational Distribution

Half the working women were in the service trades, commerce, and transport. Very few were in top jobs; career women were rare. Only a quarter of the students in higher education were women.

As in other countries, women with degrees were more likely to work than the less educated; the figure in Germany was 70 percent (61:23). Of these, almost two-thirds were teachers. The usual pattern prevailed: the largest group, 44 percent, taught in elementary or special schools, 10 percent in vocational schools, 9 percent in the secondary schools, and 1 percent in colleges and universities. Among male graduates, on the other hand, one-quarter were university teachers. The majority of women on academic staffs were at the lowest level, "teaching assistants." Scientists have done better than arts students. In 1966, for example, a woman scientist became the first female rector of Heidelberg; the previous year, a woman scientist had been made rector of the Dresden College of Technology.

The proportion of women in medicine was higher than in the United States; medicine is included among the traditional subjects fairly easily reconcilable with "woman's role." Dentistry also has a relatively substantial proportion of women, 13 percent; and pharmacy is becoming a popular choice for women (61:14, 45).

The civil service employed few women in the better jobs. Only 4 percent of the persons working in the administrative section were women. Most of the women were found in "women's sections": in health and family affairs, for example, where they were 17 percent and 9 percent of all employees.

Women deputies in parliament constituted 7 to 9 percent of the total in the period 1949 to 1969. In the committees, however, where most of the important work gets done, they numbered only about 6 percent in the same period (61:37, 42).

Attitudes. In a 1960 survey of 138 university teachers, among whom there were three women, 79 percent of the males expressed a negative attitude toward women as university teachers. When asked to give reasons for the scarcity of women in the profession, the men cited most often: lack of intelligence and creative qualities, inability to think abstractly, excessive shyness, overdependency, and lack of interest, in that order (61:32-33).

SWITZERLAND

The richest country in Europe after Sweden (75:605), Switzerland has been noted for its reluctance to enfranchise women. It may be taken, then, that traditional attitudes are strong in this country.

Labor-Force Participation Rates

It is significant that, despite a continuing postwar labor shortage leading to the employment of temporary immigrant labor from the Mediterranean countries (which has amounted to as much as one-third of the total labor force), the labor-force participation rate for Swiss women has risen only slightly, from 33 percent of all women in 1941 to 35 percent in 1960. The second peak, middle-aged female employment, remained very low: from a participation rate of 70 percent for the twenty to twenty-four-year-old age group in the 1960 census, there was a drop to 31 percent for all the age groups between thirty and sixty, with a further decline after sixty years. The percentage of married women employed, although it is still very low, did rise substantially, from 10 percent to 16 percent in the ten years 1950 to 1960.

As elsewhere, the more educated women went to work in larger numbers. The labor-force participation rate of university graduates was as high as 50 percent, according to the 1960 census. In Geneva, where more women were working than in rural areas, 11.5 percent of mothers of children under six years were employed in 1960 (28:305).

Occupational Distribution

Thirty-six percent of the economically active women were employed in industry in 1960, the largest single number in the clothing industry, and many in food and textiles (28:314). Another 20 percent were in commerce, banking, and insurance; 11 percent worked as domestic servants; and 10 percent were in other services. The female foreign workers, who constituted 30 percent of all immigrant labor, worked predominantly in hotels (14 percent) and domestic service (19 percent) (28:305).

Education and Training

In fifteen of the twenty-two Swiss cantons, girls in secondary school were taught less mathematics than were boys; in fourteen, they were given less science. The situation with respect to vocational training was similar: in the canton of Geneva, for example, 88 percent of the boys, but only 65 percent of the girls, received any training after leaving school.

The traditional occupational divisions prevailed, as they did also in apprenticeships (28:300-1).

Equal Pay

Switzerland has failed to ratify the ILO's Equal Renumeration Convention, although, incidentally, the headquarters of the ILO are in Geneva (28:307).

Among workers, women's earnings averaged 63 percent of men's in 1964; the differential among salaried workers was slightly less, 68 percent. It was rare, as late as the mid-1960s, for a woman civil servant to receive the same salary as a man. Some cantons had a salary scale with lower pay for women officials. Only six cantons, in 1965, paid women teachers at the same rate as men. As late as 1950, women were allowed to teach only the lower elementary school classes in some cantons.

In some industries, the metallurgical industry, for example, occupational classifications put women all in one group at one wage rate, regardless of skill. Pay scales would be listed for skilled, unskilled, and semiskilled workers, and then for all women who received the lowest rates regardless of skill (28:308).

Legal Discrimination

Marriage may constitute grounds for discharge from federal employment.

As a natural corollary to the inability of women to vote in most cantons until very recently, women were discriminated against in public service and in quasipublic activities, such as the law.

Taxation. A steeply progressive income tax served as a disincentive to married women's seeking employment, because husbands and wives had to file joint returns without the split-income provision in the American system.

NETHERLANDS

The Netherlands has historically been one of the most advanced countries in the world in its tolerance of political and social deviance. These are obviously quite different from relations within the family, for in this area the Netherlands is one of the most conservative countries in the West.

Labor-Force Participation Rates

In 1967 only 27 percent of all women between the ages of fifteen and sixty-five were counted as employed, including farmers' wives. Among married women, the number employed had fallen from 10 percent in 1947 to 7 percent in 1960, reflecting the decline of the population engaged in agriculture. Nevertheless, as many as half the married women employed in 1960 were still working on family farms. While the proportion of married women employed outside the home, excluding farmers' wives, doubled from 1947 to 1960, this increase involved only a rise from 2 to 4 percent (54:66).

Attitudes. The Institute for Psychological Market Research and Motivation Research conducted a questionnaire survey of almost 2,000 women in 1964, of whom 10 percent were working outside the home.[1] The majority of those interviewed opposed employment for women with family responsibilities; the more educated and higher-income women expressed less opposition than the others. According to the women, an even greater majority of husbands were opposed to their wives' working.

Occupational Distribution

One-third of the employed women in the 1964 survey mentioned above were in domestic service, and only 8 percent were in industry.

[1]Four-page summary in English obtained from the Dutch Ministry of Social Affairs.

Women supplied 52 percent of elementary school teachers in Holland in the period 1958 to 1968, but only 22 percent of the secondary school teachers and 3 percent of university staff.

Attitudes. The working women in the 1964 survey were reported to be, in general, satisfied with their jobs.

Education

Holland had the lowest rate in 1965 of female enrollment in universities of any of the OECD countries except Japan. In female graduates, its rate was lower than Japan's. It also had the smallest rate of increase in the preceding decade. Women accounted for one-fifth of the total enrollment in 1964 and even less, a bare 12 percent, of first-level degrees granted in 1966. The most popular field of study for women was the humanities.

Legal Discrimination

The legal requirement that women retire on marriage has been removed in government service and in public school teaching, but there are still clauses in private union agreements giving the employer the right to discharge a female employee if she marries. Teachers in Holland's many private schools are among those subject to such provisions. The maternity protection tax on employers, to finance compulsory maternity leaves, encourages employers to fire married women.

The government has recently merged the men's and women's sections of the public employment offices, as a symbol of desegregation (54:66).

CHAPTER 6   THE SOVIET UNION AND
THE EASTERN EUROPEAN
COMMUNIST COUNTRIES

The Soviet Union is the outstanding example of a country that has broken with tradition, of a country in which women are doctors, engineers, cosmonauts, and tractor drivers, and enjoy equal pay, equal education, abortion on demand,[1] twenty-four-hour or five-day-a-week child care centers, and the option to retain their maiden names (84). The other Eastern European communist countries lag behind, possibly because they have had less time in which to change traditional patterns of employment.

A much higher proportion of women work in the Soviet Union than in any other country. The reasons are not entirely ideological; women are needed in the labor market. Over twenty-five million men were lost in World War II, a loss which resulted not only in a high proportion of women in the working age groups, but also in a high proportion of single women who are always, in every country, more likely to seek employment than married women. The governments of the communist countries launched active campaigns to induce women to work. Women who stayed at home even to take care of their children were made to feel guilty. Wages were kept low deliberately, so that families could not live on the earnings of a single wage earner.

Girls were urged in all the mass media to emulate successful career women. They were educated and trained in the same schools and the same subjects as boys. Education was

[1]But abortion is the only available method of birth control (84:37).

heavily mathematics and science oriented; training stressed the technology of heavy industry. The result was the breaking of the old mold of women's occupations, and women entered "men's occupations" in unprecedented numbers. Medicine, even in Czarist days one of the professions open to women, became predominantly female.

The Soviet Union must be credited with a tremendous achievement in educating and training women on the same level as men. Women's preferences were not solicited; only an authoritarian regime could have accomplished so much in so short a time.

Now let us consider the other side of the coin. Entry into the labor market meant satisfying, fulfilling work for professional women; but it meant backbreaking drudgery for most women, cleaning the streets or doing heavy labor on building sites or in the fields. An American driving through Russia gave a lift to a collective farm worker and, in introducing his wife, added that she also worked. The answer from the old woman was: "You're fooling me. You can't tell me that women have to work in a rich country like America."

Women in Russia are still responsible for the home and the care of the children. Housekeeping involves long hours of marketing because of the inefficiency of retail distribution. Many household appliances are still in short supply. Household services—laundry, dry cleaning, prepared foods—are inadequate. The provision of day care for children does not meet the demand; the grandmothers have been filling the gap.

Perhaps the heavy physical burden of two jobs and the psychological burden of responsibility for the home—when a child is sick it is still the mother who stays home—explain in part another aspect of the situation of Soviet women which is less than ideal. Women do not reach the top in numbers anywhere near their ratio to the total employed in any occupation.

The very important Communist party is almost entirely masculine at all the upper levels. Even in the women's occupations—teaching, medicine—we find the typical progression, with the number of women declining as the level of responsibility and status rises. There are still women's occupations in the Soviet Union: even in engineering women tend to concentrate on the consumer goods industries; in science they are drawn, as elsewhere, to biology and chemistry rather than physics.

Why is this? Tradition dies hard and perhaps even the fifty-six years since the October 1917 Revolution have not been long enough to effect change in basic attitudes. It is a small sign but significant that the equality of the sexes in the Soviet Union does not extend to automobile ownership, which is just becoming a possibility for many families. The automobile is still a new gadget and, apparently, a masculine privilege; a woman driving a car is not only rare but evokes lively reactions from the public (84:37).

The proportion of women among university students has begun to drop; from a high point of 53 percent in 1950, it fell to 44 percent in 1965. Is this a sign that, as the sex imbalance in the population slowly works itself out, Soviet planners will rely less in the future on highly educated woman-power?

Another statistic carries the seeds of a change in policy by the state: the birth rate among working women has fallen substantially all over the Eastern bloc. Already, in Hungary, government pressure on women to work has let up, and they are being paid to stay at home for several years after they have children. The birth rate in the Soviet Union is now lower than that of the United States. It is conceivable that the government will take alarm at the precipitous decline and reverse its policy on the employment of women.

The continuation and strengthening of the current trend towards the equality of women may, on the other hand, continue. It may be that "equal status in the family . . . and in public activity," in the hopeful words of the new Czech constitution, and further progress toward "equal status . . . at work" will come for women.

Demographic Factors and Labor Demand

In the early days, after the October 1917 Revolution in Russia, women were encouraged to go to work outside the home for ideological reasons: the communist party was opposed to the family as a bourgeois institution. Later on, as the social philosophy of the regime became more traditional, the impetus to the employment of women came, on the one hand, from the economic requirements of the drive to industrialize and, on the other hand, from the shortage of men because of the losses in World War I and in the Revolution and the civil war that followed. There was an imbalance of the sexes in the population from the beginning; then, in World War II, Russia lost about 25 million men.

The census of 1959 put the numerical predominance of women at 55 percent of the total population, but as high as 63 percent of the population aged 35 and over. (The comparable figures for the United States were 51 and 52 percent for the same year.) The population of working age in the postwar period was, therefore, composed roughly of 60 percent women. The tremendous tasks of reconstruction, the maintenance of a large standing army after World War II, and the intensive drive for economic growth made it essential that women enter the labor market in unprecedented numbers.

The other communist countries also had ambitious plans to industrialize and faced the same requirement to get women into the labor market. The German Democratic Republic was subject to imbalance of the sexes similar to, although not so great as, the Soviet Union's not only because of wartime losses, but because of the flight of refugees out of the country. In 1964 there were 119 women for every 100 men in East Germany, a disparity greater than in West Germany, where the ratio was 113 to 100 (61:65).

The demographic effects of World War II were not limited to the war casualties. The low birth rate during the war years produced very small additions to the labor force coming of age in the late 1950s and 1960s, thus maintaining the pressure on women as a source of labor.

The tremendous war losses meant, further, that millions of women were not able to marry. Although marriage does not keep women out of the labor market in Russia to the same extent as it does in the West, married women are less likely to work even in Russia; hence, the high proportion of unmarried women tended to increase the supply of women in the labor market. In fact, about half the Russian female labor force is unmarried, a larger proportion than that prevailing in many Western countries, including the United States.

Labor-Force Participation Rates

Women's activity rates are higher in the Eastern European countries than in the West, as Table 19 indicates. The greater importance of agriculture in the less-developed East accounts for part of the difference but not for all, as the figures for urban areas alone show. Note that the age range to which the rates apply is narrower than the fifteen to sixty-five range generally used in the West; the narrower range tends to raise the rates because it eliminates the leakages of women still attending school in the lower and of retirements in the upper age groups. The statutory retirement age for women in the Eastern European countries is fifty-five years (fifty for heavy occupations in the Soviet Union), except for Poland and East Germany, where it is sixty years.

The figures for married women alone are also striking. Only Finland in the West matched the 60 percent (or higher) participation rate for married women that prevailed in East Germany, Czechoslovakia, and Poland (2:185).

About 30 percent of the women workers in the Soviet Union were estimated to have children. In 1959 the labor-force participation rate for the age group twenty to thirty-nine, covering the child-bearing years, was an almost incredible 80 percent. Since then, the birth rate has declined; the extent of the fall in the crude birth rate, which has dropped from 47

Table 19:   Female Activity Rates in the 20 to 54 Age Group in Eastern
and Western European Countries
(last population census date)

Country	Total	Urban
Eastern Europe		
Bulgaria (1965)	81.5	49.6[a]
Soviet Union (1959)	76.9	
Rumania (1966)	76.7	59.6
East Germany (1964)	69.1[b]	
Poland (1960)	66.2	53.4
Czechoslovakia (1961)	63.1	
Hungary (1960)	50.2	61.3
Western Europe		
Turkey (1960)	66.0	10
Finland (1960)	58.0	61
Austria (1961)	56.3	
Western Germany (1961)	48.8	
Yugoslavia (1961)	47.7	
France (1962)	44.8	45
United Kingdom (1961)	44.0	
Greece (1961)	40.6	27
Denmark (1960)	40.2	45
Sweden (1960)	39.6	47
Switzerland (1960)	38.5	
Belgium (1961)	33.2	
Italy (1961)	32.4	
Ireland (1961)	29.6	
Norway (1960)	24.7	37
Netherlands (1960)	22.7	
Spain (1960)	18.1	22
Portugal (1960)	17.8	31

[a]1956 census data
[b]21 to 54 age group

Source: United Nations, Economic Commission for Europe, *Economic Survey of Europe, 1968* (Geneva: 1969), p. 249.

per thousand in 1913 to 19.7 in 1964 to about 16 today,[2] would undoubtedly be exceeded if age-specific rates were available.

Mothers were less likely to work, in the East as in the West, if they had young children. Labor-force participation rates

[2]The United States birth rate, for comparison, is 17.8 per thousand (79:1).

were nevertheless, extremely high, as Table 20 demonstrates for East Germany.

In general in the East, as in the West, there was a negative association between women working outside the home and the number of dependent children, although there was only a weak relation on collective farms in Russia (2:185-90).

Table 20: Economic Activity Rates among Mothers with at Least One Child under 16, East Germany, 1964

Number of children	Age of children		
	0-2	3-5	6-16
One	56.5	74.1	74.7
Two	44.8	56.9	66.9
Three	44.3	52.7	60.1
Four	43.5	49.3	54.4
Five and over	38.7	42.6	45.2
All mothers aged 18 to 49	49.2	59.1	67.2

Source: Jerzy Berent, "Some Demographic Aspects of Female Employment in Eastern Europe and the USSR," *International Labor Review,* February 1970, p. 185.

Occupational Distribution

Sizable proportions of the working women in the Eastern European countries were employed in the still large agricultural sectors of those countries. In the Soviet Union, where almost half the civilian labor force was engaged in agriculture in the early 1960s, the proportion among women workers was higher—53 percent. Fifty-six percent of collective farmers were women.

On the farms, the women supplied 61 percent of the physical labor, most of it nonspecialized and unskilled. Their overwhelming preference was for field work—planting, cultivating, harvesting—which is seasonal. They supplied swineherds, milking workers, and poultry workers. On the other hand, women numbered only 0.8 percent of the tractor and combine drivers, work that they had handled during the war but had moved out of afterwards when it became highly centralized on a regional basis and involved long periods away from home. Even on the lower levels of management, there were few women. On the higher levels, Krushchev has been quoted as remarking at a regional farm conference (10:168):

> We all know what an enormous role women play in all the sectors in the building of communism. But for some reason there are few women in this hall. Just take a pair of binoculars and have a look around. What is the reason for this? It will be said that it is mainly administrative workers who are present here. It turns out that it is the men who do the administrating and the women who do the work.

Construction and transport had very small numbers of women workers in all the Eastern countries: in construction, less than 15 percent of all workers were women in most of the countries, except Russia (28 percent); and, in transport, no more than 25 percent (2:178).

The share of women in employment in industry ranged from 47 percent in the Soviet Union in 1967 through approximately 40 percent in Bulgaria, Czechoslovakia, East Germany, and Hungary, to a low of about 30 percent in Poland, in 1966, and Rumania (2:178). As in the West, women were unevenly distributed, with heavy representation in the textile, clothing, and food-processing industries, although the proportion of women in the heavy industries was more substantial than in the West.

The largest contingent of women worked in the trade and service sectors, as in the West: in public health, credit and finance, and education. In these sectors, the proportions of women generally ranged from 50 to 75 percent in the seven Eastern European countries (2:178).

Professions. Before the 1917 Revolution in Russia, the few women in the professions were primarily in medicine and in teaching (10:74). The long tradition in Russia that care of the sick is an acceptable field for women explains, in part, the startling fact that today medicine is almost entirely a women's occupation in the Soviet Union. It is interesting, however, that surgery tends to be dominated by men, who are considered more capable of the necessary emotional detachment (10:129).

The attractiveness of working conditions in medicine in the Soviet Union is probably particularly important to women; doctors work a six-hour day (seven in the factories). There are night shifts, which men are asked to take more often than women. Because of tradition and the good conditions, it is not necessary to offer high salaries to induce students to go into medicine. The relatively low pay in turn contributes to the domination of the field by women, who now total 80 percent of all doctors. Feminine predominance in a profession seems to have exactly the same consequences in the Soviet Union as it does in the West (47:100-101).

Engineering represents another triumph for Soviet education. Although there are more women in the technology of the food and consumer goods industries than in branches of engineering such as mining or transport, the overall figure for women engineers in 1964 was 31 percent (10:194).

The Soviet record for women in medicine and engineering is not matched by other communist countries. The data for several professions in Poland, for example, compare with those for the Soviet Union and the United States as follows (60:42):

	Poland (1958)	Soviet Union (1959)	United States (1961)
Doctors	36.4	79.0	5.0
Dentists	77.0	83.0	2.0
Lawyers	18.8	37.0	3.5
Engineers	8.0	32.0	

Legal reform has recently improved the law as a field for women in East Germany. With the appointment of "people's judges," women have become magistrates—42 percent were women in 1966—and even judges—31 percent (61:108).

Among the top professional personnel in the Soviet Union, women have improved their representation. The pattern typical of women's career experiences, with the number of women falling off as prestige, responsibility, and income rise, still, however, prevails, after fifty-six years of theoretical equality (see Table 21).

Table 21:   Women Scientific Workers with Academic Titles[a]
in the Soviet Union
1950 and 1964

	Number of women		Percent of women	
	1950	1964	1950	1964
Total	16,569	42,900	26.9	32.2
Academicians, corresponding members, professors	474	1,000	5.4	8.3
Associate professors	3,226	8,800	14.8	19.1
Senior research workers	3,450	7,900	30.4	29.0
Junior research workers and assistants	9,419	25,200	48.0	52.3

Source: N. T. Dodge, *Women in the Soviet Economy* (Baltimore: Johns Hopkins, 1966), pp. 196-197, Table 115.

[a]These titles are retained although the scientists may be working in industry, government, the military, research institutes, or universities.

Semiprofessional Occupations. The Soviet Union has developed the semiprofessions to a much greater extent than any other country has. With training provided in specialized secondary schools, these occupations include nurses, medical technicians, dentists, school teachers (elementary and preschool), planners, statisticians, accountants, agronomists, and legal personnel. (See Table 22.) According to Dodge, "The proportion of women among semiprofessionals is substantially higher than among professionals. It is also higher than among workers and employees and is even higher than the proportion of women among collective farm workers" (190). These semiprofessions include the white-collar occupations in which women are also concentrated in the West, although the range is wider. They have lower incomes and status than the professions, but they also require shorter training and less commitment to a career.

Table 22: Women Semiprofessionals in the Soviet Union, 1964

	Percent distribution	Percent of total in occupation
Total female specialists	100.0	63
Technicians	24.1	38
Agronomists, etc.	4.7	44
Statisticians, planners, etc.	12.6	76
Medical personnel (including dentists)	30.3	92
Teachers, librarians, etc.	24.3	83
Other	4.0	

Source: N. T. Dodge, *Women in the Soviet Economy* (Baltimore: Johns Hopkins, 1966), p. 190, Tables 107 and 108.

Education and Training

Since the 1917 Revolution, educational opportunities have expanded greatly in the Soviet Union, for women even more than for men. Girls constituted about half the enrollment of primary and secondary schools, even in the rural areas, in the 1960s. In the upper secondary grades, in the cities, girls numbered more than half the enrollment, because boys were more likely to drop out to take a job or to enter vocational or technical schools. The curriculum is heavily science oriented and both uniform and required for both sexes.

Female enrollment in the universities rose after the Revolution until, in 1955, it reached 52 percent, which equalled the proportion of women in the population of college age at that time (10:112). After 1955, the proportion of women began to lution until, in 1955, it reached 52 percent, which equalled the decline, reaching a low in 1961 and 1962 of only 42 percent. Policies in effect from 1955 to 1965 tended to reduce the acceptance of women: preference was given to veterans and to those with employment experience nominated by industrial and farm enterprises; only one-fifth were admitted directly from secondary schools. After the employment experience requirement was lifted, the figure for women rose slightly to 44 percent in 1965.

A much smaller proportion of women, 28 percent, received candidate (Ph.D.) degrees from 1962 to 1964 and only 21 percent the higher doctoral degree, which has no equivalent in the United States (10:137). About two-thirds of the women graduate students were in public health or education (10:135).

The most popular fields of study for women university students were education and cultural subjects, medicine, and socioeconomic subjects, in that order. Trailing, but with a substantial female representation, were engineering, in which women were 30 percent of the students, and agriculture, in which they formed one-quarter.

At the level of higher degrees, the figures below are the estimated percentages of women receiving candidate degrees, by field, in the period 1962 to 1964:

Pure science		25.5
Physics, mathematics	16.8	
Chemistry	38.2	
Biology	53.2	
Geology	26.9	
Applied science		30.1
Technology	12.4	
Agriculture, veterinary medicine	28.6	
Medicine	47.0	
Nonscientific fields		25.3
Total		27.9

The same preferences that women show in the West are apparent here, although in an attenuated form; among the sciences, biology and medicine attract the most women and much less interest is shown in technological subjects.

In other Eastern countries, the proportion of women attending universities is also high compared with that in the West. In Czechoslovakia, of the Prague population twenty to twenty-four years old in the middle 1960s 3.5 percent of the men and 3.0 percent of the women were university educated (62:402). East Germany, with only 16 percent of all 1960 graduates women, was an exception. Among the new students that year, the proportion of women was 25 percent; drop-out rates in German universities are high, and particularly so among girls. The percentage of women enrolled had risen by 1968 to 32 (61:76-8).

More than half the women university students in East Germany studied medicine; the other popular subjects were the familiar languages, education, and art. The small number of women in colleges of technology also follows the familiar pattern, although the 8 percent figure for East Germany is higher than in any Western country.

Despite attempts to encourage women to undertake vocational training, three-quarters of all women workers in the German Democratic Republic were reported to be unskilled, compared with 30 percent of the men (61:74).

Women's Attainments

The participation of women in education and the widening of the range of women's occupation which have been characteristic of the Soviet experience, are, of course, outstanding. Unfortunately, an evaluation of the achievement of women, trained now to undertake every type of economic and professional activity open to men, reveals a disappointing record of indifferent success. In the other countries of Eastern Europe, with much less achievement in educating and training women and less change in tradition, the final results are also less impressive than in the Soviet Union.

In most branches of the economy in the Soviet Union, the proportion of women among the "leading personnel," managerial and technical people, is substantially lower than their representation among all workers. Only in public health and education have women reached the top jobs in numbers almost proportionate to their relative strength (10:201). Even within education, the disparities grow as the levels rise. In higher educational institutions, women were less successful than in the elementary and secondary school systems. In 1960 they filled 41 percent of the lowest positions (instructor and so forth) and were one-quarter of the associate professors, 11 percent of the professors, 9 percent of the deans, 12 percent of department heads, and 5 percent of the directors and deputy directors of institutes (10:207). Similarly, among heads of medical establishments, only 57 percent were women, although women made up 82 percent of physicians without administrative functions (10:209).

The top élite of the scientific and intellectual world is identified by membership in the Academy of Sciences. In the mid-1960s, 2 percent of academicians and 2.6 percent of corresponding members were women. And these few were not among the influential, active members (10:219 *ff.*). The role of women is slightly larger in some of the specialized academies. For example, out of a membership of 104 in the Academy of Medical Science in 1964 four were women and of 142 corresponding members 13 were women.

Politics, a much more pervasive aspect of life in the communist countries than in the West, has remained a man's field. Women constituted 20 percent of the members of the party in 1961; but only 10 women belonged to the Central Committee of the Communist party of the Soviet Union, 3.1 percent of the membership, and there were no female members of the top politbureau. Participation of women in high governmental posts is also rare and mainly restricted to cultural, educational, and health positions (10:214).

Among the other communist countries, the record is more like the West's. In East Germany, for example, the figures for women university teachers make it very clear that the masculine tradition still holds—16 percent of the university graduates were women in 1960, but only 4 percent of teaching staff; five years later women professors were still only 5 percent (61:105). One-third of the junior staff, however, were women. It is interesting to observe that, among women, scientists had the greatest success in reaching the highest ranks. It is also interesting that the successful women were more likely to remain single; about half the women faculty were unmarried. Of those who were married, half had no children; and among the families with children, one child was the norm.

In the German Democratic Republic, the "masculine" structure of industry had not changed. There were limited prospects for promotion within industry for women, not only because of inadequate qualifications but also because of a new factor more important than in the West: political activity. Fewer women than men were Communist party members and, while not required, party membership was commonly associated with holding the best jobs. A study of women's career prospects in East Germany found great improvement, which did not yet, however, amount to equality. On the average, the study concluded, while one male graduate in three was appointed to a senior post in the government, the party, or industry, the ratio for women was one in nineteen (61:112).

In Poland, comparative figures indicate that women in industry were less successful than in the Soviet Union (60:41):

Proportion of Women Managers in Industry in Poland (1958) and the Soviet Union (1961)

	Poland	Soviet Union
Director of plants	2.1	6.0
Chief engineers	2.1	16.0
Heads of production units	6.0	24.0
Heads of economic units	15.2	33.0
Head bookkeepers	20.0	33.0
Economists	39.3	76.0

Equal Pay

It must be clear by now that women hold low-wage jobs, on the whole, in Eastern Europe as well as in the West. In Czechoslovakia, for example, average earnings for women were estimated to be one-third lower than for men (62:406). In Poland, we are told, women may earn substantially less even when they work in the same occupations as men, with identical education and experience (60:37).

Child Care

There were places in kindergartens and weekly boarding schools in the German Democratic Republic for 45 percent of the children between three and six years old in 1967 and in nurseries for 20 percent of the children under three; but these were not sufficient to satisfy the need. Over half of all mothers with two or more children worked, and three-quarters of those with only one child between three and six (61:97). Provisions for child care in the other countries were considerably less than adequate (2:191, n.1).

In the Soviet Union, there were nurseries in the mid-1960s to accommodate 12 percent of the children from two months to three years old. Supervision was provided at playgrounds in the rural areas during the farming seasons for almost an equal number. Kindergartens provided places for about 20 percent of the total number of preschool children of three years or over. At both nurseries and kindergartens, children could be boarded overnight for the week. These institutions are not free; payment is on a sliding scale depending on income. The demand exceeded the supply and there were plans to expand child care further. Many, if not most, preschool children of working mothers were being cared for by their grandmothers or other old people.

Future Prospects

The active measures taken by Eastern European governments to stimulate the employment of women in economic activity outside the home were, as we noted above, dictated largely by demographic imbalances, which limited the supply of men, and by the demand for labor.

Implicit in these policies was the assumption that women who stayed at home were making less of a contribution to society. Nevertheless, the long work day that women with a job have to put in, because of the extra three to four-and-a-half hours a day required by housekeeping duties,[3] has taken its toll in reduced productivity. Hence, since the long-term

---

[3] "Comrade's Lib.," an article by Neil Ulman in the *Wall Street Journal*, January 16, 1971, describes the elderly women who took time off from snow shoveling for a catnap in the warmth of a staircase in a large department store. "Since women work hard, nobody is surprised if they get tired."

development plans of most of the communist countries include the use of female labor on an expanded scale, the production of household appliances is generally being increased; and the development of public catering, to relieve women of cooking, is an increasingly recognized need (62:408-9).

Factors have emerged, however, that may well change government policy on the employment of married women. First, the relative scarcity of men will disappear as the population ratio evens out over time. This increase in the number of men also means that the proportion of married women is going to increase. Second, there was a dramatic fall in the birth rate all over Eastern Europe beginning in the mid-1950s. In Hungary, the contribution of women's employment to the falling birth rate has been recognized, and steps have already been taken to reverse the trend. Government payments, for example, are now made to women for some years after childbirth, provided they stop working (2:191).

In Czechoslovakia, a conference of sociologists in 1964 found a contradiction in contemporary socialist societies "between women's emancipation and economic activity on the one hand and their biological and social functions on the other." This "contradiction" will probably gain increasing consideration from government planners.

According to a Reuters dispatch,[4] there are many studies being made in Eastern Europe of the falling birth rate and rising divorce rates, fatigue, and the infertility of working women. There is some evidence, on the other hand, that the Soviet Union, which has the highest economic participation rate of women now, may attempt in the future to push it even higher. A recent work on demographic aspects of employment, written by members of the Research Institute of the Soviet Planning Commission, estimated that women's presence at home was needed for one-and-a-half to two years after pregnancy. On this basis, they calculated the possible limit of the labor-force participation rate of women aged sixteen to fifty-five, which was 79 percent in 1965, at somewhere in the range of 86 to 90 percent (2:192). It will be interesting to see if this rate is achieved or if, with a falling birth rate and with increasing affluence, the planners reduce the pressure on women to enter the labor market—or if the women themselves begin to resist the pressure.

⁴*The New York Times*, Nov. 1, 1971, p. 56.

Conclusions

With higher proportions of women in the labor market than in the West, and with an ideological commitment to "equality," the Soviet Union has enforced radical changes in the employment of women, but has not yet succeeded in changing completely the basic social situation. Even when training is available to women, they prefer, for whatever reason, the traditional women's occupations—taking care of people, the sick and children—which are generally the less-skilled occupations and among the lowest paid. The outstanding exception is medicine which is, in the Soviet Union, one of the women's occupations; and even this profession, when it is dominated by women, becomes a low-income occupation. Even in the women's occupations, women are not often found in top jobs.

> Although the prospects for a woman entering and succeeding in a professional career in the Soviet Union appear to be much more favorable than in the United States or in other Western countries, the prospects for advancement are not equally favorable. The proportion of women in the administrative and professional jobs, although much higher now than before World War II, tends to decrease with each successive increase in rank, even in such fields as education and health, where the role of women is dominant. The same pattern holds in the fields of science and technology where women are less important. There appears to be an undeniable tendency for female specialists in all fields to congregate in the lower and middle echelons. Perhaps the most striking instance of this is the small number of women among the [Communist] party professionals, but it holds to a lesser degree in all other areas of activity (10:214-5).

The Soviet regime was formed in 1917. The other Eastern European countries have had a much shorter communist span—they began either during World War II or shortly after the war—and have seen less change in the traditional attitudes towards women and within women themselves. These countries seem very similar to many of the Western countries with dual labor markets. We are told, for example, that in the German Democratic Republic, despite large-scale attempts to assist women through education and training which approach discrimination in their favor, the "masculine structure" of industry, of the universities, of the Communist party, and of the government has not changed (61:112). In the Czech Constitution of 1960, there is a clause stating the full equality of the sexes—"equal status in the family, at work, and in public activity"—but one writer asserted that "it cannot be claimed that everything has already been done to implement article 27. . . ." (62:397-98). She added that "any genuine analysis must also take into account that even in our socialist society there are tendencies to give preference to men, rather than women, in spite of equal training or skills, in appointments to jobs that entail executive or administrative ability. . . ." (62:406-7).

In Poland where, we have learned, "wages of men and women, working in the same occupations, holding the same posts, with identical situation and experience, very often differ substantially . . . ," the writer asserted that "the complicated process of reconciling the problems of employment with the popular image of the female sex . . . is causing upheavals in all aspects of both individual and community life, and cannot be a matter of indifference to anyone" (60:37).

The Dual Burden. The one element in the situation that is accepted as incontrovertable is that women have the principal responsibility for home and children. The implications of this fact are larger than the mere time involved, although that is a considerable factor.

The conflict faced by career women in our society, the fear of appearing unfeminine, does not exist in the Soviet Union where the hardworking, productive career woman is forcefully and frequently presented in the mass media as the model for young women to emulate. Nevertheless, conflict of another kind does exist, and that is the conflict between the demands of the job and the demands of the home—in the form of long queues for marketing after work and the hours required for housekeeping duties or for caring for a sick child or even a sick husband at home.

A Russian writer pointed out recently that surveys have shown that Russian women do not want to quit working. Nevertheless, although all doors are open to women, including the door "upstairs," not many go through them. She denied the common explanations that women show less initiative than men or preferred less taxing work; she admitted that they took sick leave more often and were less mobile when it came to taking new assignments away from home. She charged that some men, even in the Soviet Union, dislike seeing women get top jobs. The principal reason for women's limited success, she asserted, was the double burden of work on women at home and on the job.

> A vicious circle arises. Being tired, a woman selects mechanical work. And such work does not stimulate creative thinking and, therefore, has less pay. So the main role of family provider falls to the husband. Tacitly, this comes to mean that the wife is expected to do the overwhelming part of the housework (an article in *Literaturnaya Gazeta,* quoted in 58:56; see also 60:43, and 62:407).

Productivity. Norton Dodge investigated systematically the reasons for the failure of women in the Soviet Union to win promotions in proportion to their numbers. The Russians, he found, had done no research on the question for at least two reasons. First, they accept on faith that social and environmental factors favor complete equality for women. No one admits to prejudice against women, as workers or as bosses, and Dodge believed that prejudice did not, as such exist. Second, prevailing attitudes and policies, which have a philosophical underpinning of materialism and thus tend to ignore biological, psychological, emotional, and other factors, rule out the possibility of any study on differences between the sexes.

Dodge did some research on one aspect of this question: the productivity of women workers, with a view to assessing the economic rationality of the distribution of women in the employment hierarchy. The facts will not tell us *why* women are less productive, if such is the case, but they are indeed relevant to the question and help to narrow it down. Dodge (215) argued that if women "are as competent and as productive as men, yet are not employed in positions commensurate with their capacities, wasteful use is being made of them. If, on the other hand, their competence or productivity is less, there is an economic rationale for the employment of a smaller proportion of women in the higher ranks."

Contributions to Scholarly Literature. One method used by Dodge was to count the number of male and female contributors of articles to leading professional journals in fields for which he had information on the percentage of women professionals. The use of separate surname suffixes for women in Russian made this procedure possible.

Table 23 gives the proportion of women in professional fields and the proportion of women contributors to scholarly journals and shows clearly that the latter is smaller. In most of the fields, however, there was an improvement in the ratio from 1940 to 1960.

These data included people in operating jobs who would not ordinarily publish. A similar comparison was made for higher educational institutions—universities and research institutes—the personnel of which would be expected to publish. Table 24 shows similar results, with women's contributions relatively lower than their numerical importance in the field. The ratio was higher in chemistry, medicine, biology,

Table 23: Percentage of Women with Higher Education in Various Specialties Compared with Percentage of Articles in Related Professional Journals Contributed by Women, Soviet Union, 1940 and 1960

Specialists	1940				1960			
	Percentage of women in specialty	Percentage of articles by women	Ratio	Sample size	Percentage of women in specialty	Percentage of articles by women	Ratio	Sample size
Engineers, including geology	15	4	0.27	(868)	29	9	0.31	(1,877)
Agronomists, zoo technicians, veterinarians, and foresters	25	15	0.60	(430)	39	24	0.62	(676)
Agronomists	n.a.	16	—	(156)	41	25	0.61	(345)
Veterinarians	16	6	0.38	(274)	31	16	0.52	(331)
Economists, statisticians, and trade specialists	31	9	0.29	(168)	57	12	0.21	(447)
Judges, procurators, and lawyers	15	6	0.40	(121)	32	10	0.36	(203)
Physicians, excluding dentists	60	24	0.40	(203)	75	39	0.52	(549)

Source: N. T. Dodge, *Women in the Soviet Economy* (Baltimore: Johns Hopkins, 1966), p. 227.

Table 24: Percentage of Women on the Professional Staffs of Higher Educational Institutions in 1947 Compared With Percentage of Articles in Related Professional Journals Contributed by Women, Soviet Union, 1940 and 1960

Discipline	1947 Percentage of women in field	1940± Percentage of articles by women	1940± Sample size	1950± Percentage of articles by women	1950± Sample size	1960± Percentage of articles by women	1960± Sample size
Physics, mathematics	21.1	11	(247)	11	(653)	7	(1270)
Chemistry	45.3	26	(206)	32	(222)	40	(320)
Biology	47.8	26	(384)	31	(435)	36	(565)
Geology	23.4	9	(186)	23	(141)	25	(315)
Engineering	10.5	4	(868)	5	(2203)	9	(1877)
Agriculture	23.0	14	(156)	25	(294)	21	(409)
Veterinary medicine	22.3	6	(274)	7	(302)	16	(331)
Medicine	48.0	24	(203)	37	(488)	39	(549)
Physical culture	27.6	9	(127)	7	(174)	13	(115)
Social-political and philosophy	31.0	8	(131)	6	(145)	10	(180)
Economics	16.3	9	(168)	12	(288)	11	(447)
History	30.1	21	(154)	15	(178)	14	(188)
Geography	28.7	9	(105)	15	(194)	12	(125)
Philology	67.7	24	(134)	29	(120)	21	(227)
Arts	34.0	11	(216)	28	(197)	37	(207)
Law	12.7	6	(121)	7	(123)	10	(203)
Pedagogy	40.0	22	(294)	20	(348)	26	(639)
Total	35.0	16	(3974)	19	(6505)	19	(7967)

Source: N. T. Dodge, Women in the Soviet Economy (Baltimore: Johns Hopkins, 1966), p. 228.

and the arts—among the most popular fields for women—than in areas with smaller percentages of women.

Motivation. Dodge (232-33) detected in interviews with Russian women a tendency for some of them to stop short of the more responsible jobs for which their training and experience qualified them because, as we have seen above, family interests and responsibilities made the necessary commitment very difficult. Many women in the Soviet Union apparently withdraw voluntarily from the competition with men for the top jobs.

Working Life. Another factor affecting the total lifetime productivity of women is time lost because of pregnancy, illness, family responsibilities, and earlier retirement. The statutory pregnancy leave is sixteen weeks, but this is a minimum. Women also take more sick leave (10:233); and the normal retirement age for women is fifty-five years, compared with sixty for men. Moreover, the evidence is that women, in Russia at least, tend to withdraw from the labor market more rapidly *before* the normal retirement age than men (10:234).

Allowing for these factors, in addition to the lower overall participation rates of women in the labor market, Dodge (234) estimated that over her lifetime a woman with professional training may be expected to contribute at least 13 to 14 percent less work than a man.

Planning Problems. The difficulty of assigning women to jobs that involve travel or work away from home has been observed in the West. In the Soviet Union, this problem confronts the centralized control organs and extends to all specialist, professional, and managerial posts. Both the initial assignment of graduates to jobs and their subsequent job changes are controlled by different organs of the Communist party.

Separation of husband and wife is avoided, and this practice generally means that the mobility of women is limited, to the detriment of their careers. Unmarried women present other problems. The case of doctors has received a good deal of publicity. Since most doctors are women and a proper geographical distribution of doctors is enforced by the authorities in the Soviet Union, young women are often assigned to remote, perhaps very primitive, rural areas. One young woman doctor with influential parents—her mother was also a doctor—claimed to be ill when she was assigned to eastern Siberia. The grounds were first malaria, then secondary anemia; finally, the mother considered having her daughter adjudged insane, but gave up the idea as impracticable. The father, manager of a fruit tree nursery, cooperated by claiming that his daughter's presence was essential to the horticulture of the area. When the story appeared in a Russian newspaper, the girl had yet to leave for Siberia (10:235-6).

Summary. The consistently lower level of achievement of women prevails, even more strongly, at the highest levels. There are no women directors in the Academy of Sciences, and only a few full or corresponding members. Few women have high positions in the many research institutes of the academy. Women have won few Lenin prizes, and those that have are usually members of large research teams. As contributors of scholarly articles, women do somewhat better, but still less well than their numbers in the different fields would lead one to predict.

There are indications that the situation has been improving. Nevertheless, for the 1960s, Dodge concluded that highly educated Russian women were, in fact, less productive than men and that, from an economic standpoint, the filling of most of the higher posts by men was the most efficient allocation of scholarly manpower resources.

CHAPTER 7 CONCLUSIONS

This brief review of the experience of women at work has perhaps served to indicate that women are not "equal" in the labor market anywhere. The fairly common belief in the United States that women are better off in Sweden or Finland —or any other country for that matter—is mistaken.

In some aspects of women's lives, Finland does indeed seem to be very advanced. Half the university students in Finland are women, the largest proportion in the world. Over half the married women are employed, the peak activity rate in the West. Yet the occupational distribution of women is not very different in Finland than in the other Western countries. A substantial proportion of the women work in a relatively small number of occupations—"women's occupations" employing a preponderance of women workers. The participation of women in the professions is disappointingly low, apart from the medical and health professions in which Finland, along with several other European countries, far excels the United States.

In Sweden, too, the picture looks rosier at first impression. The government has accepted, in principle, a radical solution to all the problems of women, including elimination of the dual labor market. It has adopted the view of an advanced group of intellectuals that equality for women requires nothing less than the total elimination of sex-differentiation roles: men and women must share equally in every phase of family and working life, in bringing up the children, washing the dishes, and earning the family income. The government has taken two kinds of action. First, in order to counter traditional attitudes as early as possible before they tend to rigidify, the educational authorities have modified the elementary school curriculum to require that both boys and girls take courses in shop and cooking, child care and metalwork, needlework and woodwork. The other governmental action was the direction of Sweden's active labor-market policy, formulated many years ago to encourage the mobility of workers in a tight labor market, toward an attempt to expand the range of employment opportunities for women. The results of the change in the school curriculum cannot be evaluated yet; the results of the activities of the labor-market agency have been modest.

It is clear, however, that the statement of a revolutionary social position is quite a different matter from its adoption in practice; foreigners should not be misled. A segregated labor market still persists in Sweden, and social attitudes on women's place remain fairly conservative—although less conservative, we are told, than in Finland (p. 68 above).

Even in the Soviet Union, after fifty-six years of a new social order, there is less equality for women at the top, in the best jobs, than at the bottom. A disproportionate number of women work in unskilled occupations, many of them engaged in heavy manual labor. Consider the implications of the refusal of the Russian farm woman to believe the American visitor who told her that his wife worked too: "You can't tell me that in a rich country like America the women have to work."

Unequal Pay. In all countries, without exception, women fill, in the main, the low-paid jobs. Whether a country has signed the International Labor Organization convention guaranteeing equal pay for equal work—as most of them have— or has a statute on the books to the same effect, seems to make no difference, with the possible exception, in a few countries, of employment in civil service. Where men and women do the same work, the women generally earn lower rates of pay. More often, however, the women perform different work from that of the men so that it is a simple matter to call it less valuable. Even when job evaluations are made on an ostensibly objective basis, they can be manipulated to produce the right results. Even in China, we learn from a rare critical statement by the widow of Sun Yat-sen, "there are people's communes where women receive less pay for equal work."[1]

Professions. The professions, which comprise many of the most prestigious and highly paid occupations, are predominately male in every country. Nevertheless, the United States comes off rather badly here: all ten countries in Table 5 (p. 24) have a higher percentage of women in medicine than does the United States. Dentistry and pharmacy also engage a high proportion of women in some countries. The proportion of women lawyers, while typically lower than the comparable figures for doctors, is also higher in several other countries than in the United States.

Within the professions, one observes an apparently universal phenomenon: women cluster, invariably, at the bottom. From solicitor to barrister to judge, the proportion of women at each step declines. Most women doctors abroad are general practitioners not consultants or hospital chiefs.

The pyramid is the universal symbol for women, with great numbers at the base which fall away as the scale ascends, whether one considers skill, responsibility, prestige, or financial reward. Thus women are the majority of the elementary school teachers in most countries, a smaller proportion of the secondary school teachers, and a very small percentage of university teachers. (In the proportion of women in university teaching, this country ranks first, although this ranking is in part attributable to a difference in definition: we include home economics, education, and social work as university courses and most European countries do not.) Within university faculties, there is also a progression with a high proportion of women at the research assistant and instructor level and

[1]*The New York Times,* February 27, 1972, p. 31.

successively smaller percentages as the ranks ascend, up to the very few at the full professor level.

We also find the pyramid in the figures for academic degrees. Even in Finland, women receive less than half the first university degrees, and many fewer of the second and third advanced degrees. In schools, even girls' schools, women constitute the teaching staff but are rarely the principals. In the Russian academies, over half the junior and senior research workers are women, but less than one-fifth the professors, corresponding members, and academicians. In Russian agriculture, as Krushchev pointed out, the men do the administrating and the women the work. In every civil service, women are concentrated at the lower grades. In private industry in the West and the state-owned factories in the East, the number of women plant directors is very small.

Politics and Unionism

One other element in women's activity in society should be noted. Women have, until now, left politics to the men and they have not been generally active in trade unions. Their underrepresentation in these spheres of influence, both of them important centers of power, serves to reduce further their position in the labor market—or at least fails to furnish support to them in the work place. As a result, the male-dominated unions in the West have rarely waged active fights to win equal pay for women; they are at best lukewarm, at worst positively hostile to equal pay. The fact that politics remains a male bailiwick may be one significant reason for the slow progress of women in the communist countries, where the influence of the communist parties is so pervasive.

Status of Women. The status of women is a complex phenomenon, composed of many strands, and we are aware that the labor market is only part of the story. Political progressivism in a country does not seem to guarantee liberal attitudes towards married women working: the examples of Holland and Norway are sufficient to prove that. On the other hand, it would be rash to contradict the prevailing opinion in those two countries that women have a high status there.[2]

Many European men, and many women too, believe that married women should not work, particularly if there are children at home. They would be unmoved by the estimate of economists, here and abroad, that gross national product could be raised at least a quarter if women participated in the labor market to the same degree as men and all sex discrimination were abolished, because they would oppose the change in the pattern and quality of life that would ensue.[3] Many of them, and others as well, fear the effect on very small children of extended absences of their mothers; this is another question for which there is, at present, no conclusive answer.

There are, finally, many women who, in the absence of financial need, simply prefer not to work. Many men would of course make the same choice, if they had the chance. These women—and men—would deny vigorously that the status of the leisured women was lowered thereby. They can

---

[2] It may be that a seemingly trivial association affords a reliable clue to the status of women: the apparently widespread assumption, most recently evidenced in the Soviet Union, that the man of the family has an inalienable right to drive the family car. By this criterion, American women do come out way ahead of women in other countries.

[3] For Sweden, the estimate runs as high as 50 percent (72:11). In France, the rise in standards of living if women were as active as men has been put at 35 percent. Some economists favor including the value of housewives' services in the national accounts. In a careful empirical study of the time spent on work in the home by the members of almost 1,300 families, Professor Kathryn Walker of the New York State College of Human Ecology, Department of Consumer Economics and Public Policy, provided the data for the pricing of such services, which is currently being undertaken by her and by Professor William Gauger. The inclusion in GNP of work done without pay at home would, of course, raise the figure considerably. Nevertheless, the housework continues to get done, although perhaps less thoroughly, by the woman who goes out to work—she works at two jobs, putting in longer hours or, more rarely, she hires a substitute. In any case, therefore, whether housework was included in national income or not, work by women outside the home would raise GNP.

point to the fact, observed in the United States (3) but probably true in the other countries as well, that women are assigned their husband's social status and may be accorded higher status as wives than as working women, except for the rare cases of very successful women.

Discrimination or Choice? The answer to the question we asked in the first chapter seems to be: both.

It is not difficult to find the evidence for discrimination; men are often open about their prejudices. The Englishman who considered that his birthright protected him from the humiliation of working under a black or a woman represents a substantial body of male opinion. For the Soviet Union, we lack sufficient evidence to know whether the official position—complete equality—prevails in fact as well as in theory. Dodge accepted the denials of the men and women at face value, in the course of his interviews, but another (friendly) expert on the Soviet Union conceded, on the other hand, that the charge of prejudice had some validity (37:265). We have, moreover, the testimony of a Russian woman in a letter to the editor of a journal that some men dislike seeing women get top jobs, although this was not her main explanation of women's lack of achievement, as we have seen above (p. 99).

Further evidence for discrimination lies in the generalizations commonly made about women workers. They are mainly hostile, the sort of myths that plague all minorities. Women workers have been described as irritable, ruthless, nagging, whining—by women; both men and many women considered women less capable than men. Women were described as too diffident, but also, if they were successful, as too aggressive. Note that these prejudices were not voiced by men alone; they were shared by women. (See p. 8 above).

The analysis of the alternative answer to the question raised—the "choice"—is more complicated. It is clear that the segregated labor market rests on women's preferences, in the sense that no overt force dictates their choice or more precisely the series of choices that begin at fairly early ages.

Women's choice of traditional female occupations can be traced back in many cases to their school years, when they elected arts subjects rather than science or mathematics. Sometimes this "streaming" was the school's choice and not the student's. In either case, there is much to be said for the Russian system of prescribing the same science- and mathematics-oriented curriculum for both sexes, although this is contrary to the trend in the United States these days.

Later on, the young women generally took unskilled jobs upon leaving school, instead of opting for vocational training, or they took short courses in hairdressing, typing, or cooking. When they went on to universities, in relatively smaller numbers than men, they again tended to elect majors in the humanities—for which the principal career outlet is teaching, a woman's occupation at the elementary level. The fact is that most young women are looking forward to marriage and the family that follows. They expect to leave the labor market at that time, and, since most of them do not look beyond that point, any extended vocational training seems to make little sense for them.

What lies behind this "choice"? Is it only a realistic acceptance of prevailing prejudices? Probably not. Whether the decision to follow the feminine pattern is conditioned by social pressure at an early age or by biological factors at an even earlier stage is the fundamental question. But it is one to which there is at present no conclusive answer.

As we have seen, the pattern has changed since World War II with the increasing return to the labor market of married women when their children are grown. This significant development may well induce other changes in turn. When girls begin to take account of the longer duration of their working years over their whole lifetime, the desirability of more specialized education or more vocational education may seem greater than it does now. It will be more obviously rational for young girls to plan. Perhaps more women will begin to make lifetime plans that will include both domestic and economic activities, at different periods.

The Dual Burden. Beyond the questions of discrimination and choice in the segregated labor market, there is another factor to consider. Unlike single women, who are likely, other things equal, to be more successful over their working lives, the probability is that married women will continue to subordinate their careers to their major commitment to their families for a long time to come. This dual burden undoubtedly reduces both their ambition and their efficiency. The ambivalence of women who fear seeming unfeminine by competing with men will probably disappear as more women enter employment. Housework will become less arduous in the European countries, where women with jobs now put in several extra hours of housework, as they follow the American path of development and acquire more consumer durables. Even in the United States, an increase in supporting services could ease the dual burden of job and home. The main responsibility for the care of the children, however, will remain the mother's in all probability—because most women will want it that way.

The inadequacy of day-care facilities will not constitute a serious deterrent. Today there is a large unsatisfied demand even in the countries with the best facilities, but women have been resourceful in making their own informal arrangements. The informal "dayhomes," as they are called in Norway, will no doubt continue to increase as the demand expands. Even so there is always the intractable problem of the sick child—or the sick husband; the effect on women's career decisions of the mere anticipation of this problem is substantial.

In short, many women withdraw from competition for the top jobs because they do not have the time or the single-minded, undistracted concentration to devote to them. The Russian letter writer quoted earlier described, succinctly, the vicious circle: because women have other responsibilities, they content themselves with less demanding jobs, which also pay less. If the husband's earnings are higher than the wife's, his job will be considered more important than hers, by both of them, when it comes to decisions about where to live or who is to be responsible for the housework and the children. And so it will continue for a long time to come.

The Future. Social forces move slowly. Women's economic activity will probably continue to rise, but there will be no revolution. We must recognize that many women, perhaps a majority, are satisfied with the status quo. In their generally inferior jobs, with low pay, they are more satisfied than men are, or so the few surveys that have been made indicate. If women continue to be satisfied, there is little likelihood of any sudden change in their relative status in the labor market.

One qualification is an overriding consideration: full employment and economic growth are essential prerequisites for the continued advance in women's labor-force participation. In a declining market, women will tend to be pushed out, as they were in the depression of the 1930s.

If there is full employment and economic growth, the projection of current trends indicates a more than proportionate increase in the service sector, which includes many of the jobs that have traditionally been in women's sphere. School teaching may be an exception; the demand for teachers will not rise if birth rates continue to fall, as they have started to do in the United States and Eastern Europe. The falling birth rates will, at the same time, of course, encourage the tendency of women to seek work; and the opportunities in the other services besides teaching, especially the demand for health—physical and psychological—services, will be expanding.

The growth of the service sector may absorb the increased supply of women who want to work, but we should note that it also raises a disturbing alternative possibility. Growth in that sector will be at the expense of agriculture, forestry, mining, and manufacturing in which men have predominated. If overall growth rates are not sufficiently high to insure full employment for both men and women, the result may well be that men will move in and take over some of the traditionally feminine fields.

Conclusion Any job can be done by a woman. The Soviet Union has produced women astronauts, pilots (Scandinavian Airlines also has them), and miners. There are women prime ministers and truck drivers. Will the great majority of women continue to restrict themselves to the conventional women's work——whether from preference, timidity, or ignorance makes no difference—or will they break out of the mold?

Even if women continue to be less ambitious than men, less wholeheartedly committed to careers, they can nevertheless do better than they are doing now—if they want to. If they continue to be satisfied with unskilled jobs with relatively low pay because they pass the time and yield useful supplements to family earnings, nothing will change.

The influence of the new militancy in Women's Liberation groups on the vast majority of women is hard to gauge. There need not be a revolution, however; even within the present environment there is room at the top for talented or determined women—in many fields, if not in all, in every country. It is largely up to the women themselves. No one, at this time, can predict the outcome.

REFERENCES

1. Auvinen, Riitta. "Attitudes sociales et carrières féminines." *Problèmes politiques et sociaux,* 28 aout-4 septembre 1970, pp. 8-13.
2. Berent, Jerzy. "Some Demographic Aspects of Female Employment in Eastern Europe and the USSR." *International Labor Review,* February 1970, pp. 175-92.
3. Bernard, Jesse. *Academic Women.* University Park: Pennsylvania State University Press, 1964.
4. British Federation of University Women. *Graduate Women at Work.* Edited by C. Arreger. N.p.: Oriel Press, 1966.
5. Coote, Anna. "The Under-Privileged Majority." *The Observer* [London], February 7, 1971, p. 21.
6. Coxhead, Elizabeth. *Women in the Professions.* London: published for the British Council by Longmans, Green and Company, 1961.
7. Craig, Christine. *The Employment of Cambridge Graduates.* Cambridge: Cambridge University Press, 1963.
8. Dahlstrom, Edmund, ed. *The Changing Roles of Men and Women.* London: Gerald Duckworth and Co., Ltd., 1967.
9. Danish National Institute of Social Research. *Gifte Kvinder I Familie Og Ehrverv* [Married Women, Family and Work]. Vol. I. Copenhagen: Danish National Institute of Social Research, 1969.
10. Dodge, N. T. *Women in the Soviet Economy.* Baltimore: Johns Hopkins, 1966.
11. Faith, Nicholas. "Some of My Best Friends Are Women." *The Sunday Times* [London], February 21, 1971.
12. Finland, Central Statistical Bureau. *Census of Population.* Helsinki: Central Statistical Bureau, 1960. Vol. 9.
13. _____. *Statistical Yearbook.* Helsinki: Central Statistical Bureau, 1970.

14. Fogarty, Michael, A. J. Allen, Isobel Allen, Patricia Walters. *Women in Top Jobs.* London: George Allen and Unwin Ltd. for Political and Economic Planning (PEP), 1971.

15. Fogarty, Michael, Rhona Rappoport, and Robert N. Rappoport. *Women and Top Jobs.* London: George Allen and Unwin, Ltd., for PEP, 1967.

16. Great Britain General Register Office. *Sample Census 1966.* Economic Activity Tables, Part I. London: HMSO, 1968.

17. _____. Central Statistical Office. *Social Trends.* No. 1. London: HMSO, 1970.

18. Guélaud-Léridon, Françoise. *Le travail des femmes en France.* Institut national d'études démographiques et Commissariat général au plan d'équipement et de la productivité, cahier no. 42. N.p.: Presses Universitaires de France, 1964.

19. Guilbert, Madeleine. "Les effets de l' évolution technique." *Problèmes politiques et sociaux,* 28 aout-4 septembre 1970, pp. 4-7.

20. Haavio-Mannila, Elina. "The Position of Finnish Women: Regional and Cross-National Comparison." *Journal of Marriage and Family,* May 1969, pp. 339-47.

21. _____. "Research Report." *Progress: The Unilever Quarterly* 54:125-28.

22. Hanna, Vincent. "Equal Pay: Industrial Apartheid as Firms Evade the Act." *The Sunday Times* [London], November 21, 1971: p. 65.

23. _____. Part Two, November 28, 1971, p. 61.

24. Holter, Harriet. "Women's Occupational Situation in Scandinavia." *International Labor Review,* April 1966, pp. 383-400.

25. Hunt, Audrey. *A Survey of Women's Employment: A Government Social Survey Carried Out On Behalf of the Ministry of Labor in 1965.* 2 vols. March 1968. Vol 1. *Report.*

26. Institut national de la statistique et des études économiques. "Résultats préliminaire du recensement de 1968." *Economie et statistique,* 2 juin 1969, pp. 40-43.

27. James, Edward. "Women at Work in Twentieth Century Britain." *Manchester School of Economic and Social Studies,* September 1962, p. 283.

28. Janjic, Marion. "Women's Employment and Conditions of Work in Switzerland." *International Labor Review,* September 1967, pp. 292-317.

29. Jefferys, M. and P. M. Elliott. *Women in Medicine.* London: Office of Health Economics, May 1966.

30. Klein, Viola. *Britain's Married Women Workers.* London: Routledge and Kegan Paul, 1965.

31. _____. "The Demand for Professional Woman Power." *British Journal of Sociology,* June 1966, pp. 183-97.

32. Kreps, Juanita. *Sex in the Marketplace: American Women at Work.* Baltimore: Johns Hopkins, 1971.

33. Leijon, Anna-Greta. *Swedish Women-Swedish Men.* N.p.: The Swedish Institute for Cultural Relations with Foreign Countries, 1968.

34. Leser, C.E.V. "Trends in Women's Work Participation." *Population Studies* 12 (1958-59): 100.

35. _____. "Men and Women in Industry." *Economic Journal* 62 (1952): 326.

36. Likelønnsradet [Council of Equal Pay]. *De Gifte Kvinners Yrkesaktivitet Sett i Sammenheng Med Familiestruktur og Utdanning* [Married Women's Economic Activity in Relation to Family Structure and Education]. Oslo: Kommunal og Arbeidsdepartementet, November 1965.

37. Mandel, William M. "Soviet Women in the Work Force and Professions." *American Behavioral Scientist,* November/December 1971, pp. 255-80.

38. Michel, Andre. "Needs and Aspirations of Married Women Workers in France." *International Labor Review,* July 1966, pp. 39-53.

39. Myrdal, Alva and Viola Klein. *Women's Two Roles: Home and Work.* 2nd ed. London: Routledge and Kegan Paul, 1968.

40. Norway, Central Bureau of Statistics. *Educational Statistics, 1968.* Oslo: Central Bureau of Statistics, 1970.

41. _____. *Labor Market Statistics, 1969.* Oslo: Central Bureau of Statistics, n.d.

42. _____. *Ønsker Om og Behov for Sysselsetting Blant Gifte Kvinner* [Desire and Need for Employment Among Married Women]. Oslo: Central Bureau of Statistics, 1969.

43. _____. *Population Census, 1960.* Vols., 3, 4.

44. _____. *Statistical Yearbook, 1970.*

45. Norwegian Research Council for Science and the Humanities, Institute for Studies in Research and Higher Education. *Gymnasium Entrants and Graduates.* Oslo: Norwegian Research Council for Science and the Humanities, 1970.

46. _____. *Norwegian Students and Graduates at Institutions of Higher Education in Norway and Abroad.* Oslo: Norwegian Research Council for Science and the Humanities, 1971.

47. Oppenheimer, Valerie Kincade. *The Female Labor Force in the United States.* Population Monograph Series No. 5. Berkeley: Institute of International Studies, 1970.

48. Organization for Economic Cooperation and Development. *Employment of Women, International Seminars 1968-2.* Paris: OECD, 1970.

49. Pinder, Pauline. *Women at Work.* PEP Broadsheet 512. London: PEP, May 1969, pp. 523-654.

50. Price, Marna. "An Academic Woman Can Get to the Top —But It Takes Time." *The Daily Telegraph* [London], February 3, 1971, p. 11.

51. Rendel, Margherita *et al. Equality for Women.* Fabian Research Series 268. N.p.: Fabian Society, April 1968.

52. Routh, Guy. *Occupation and Pay in Britain 1906-60.* Cambridge: Cambridge University Press, 1965.

53. Roux, Claude, Mme. "Tendences récentes de l'activité féminine en France." *Population,* February 1970, pp. 179-94.

54. Seear, B. M. *Reentry of Women to the Labor Market.* Paris: Organization for Economic Cooperation and Development, 1971.

55. _____. "The Position of Women in Industry." Royal Commission on Trade Unions and Employer's Associations, Research Papers 11. London: HMSO, 1968.

56. Seear, Nancy, Veronica Roberts, and John Brock. *A Career for Women in Industry?* London: published for London School of Economics by Oliver and Boyd, Ltd., 1964.

57. Selid, Betty. *Women in Norway.* Oslo: The Norwegian Joint Committee on International Social Policy, in association with the Department of Cultural Relations, Royal Ministry of Foreign Affairs, 1970.